SUN BEAR

THE BOOK OF THE

VISION QUEST

PERSONAL TRANSFORMATION
IN THE WILDERNESS

STEVEN FOSTER
WITH MEREDITH LITTLE

D0910658

Prentice Hall Press • New York

147535

Grateful acknowledgment is made to the following for permission to reprint material copyrighted or controlled by them:

The Bollingen Foundation, Inc., for an excerpt from *Hero With a Thousand Faces* by Joseph Campbell. Doubleday & Company, Inc., for an excerpt from "Once More, The Round," copyright ©1962 by Beatrice Roethke, Administratix of the Estate of Theodore Roethke, from the book *The Collected Poems of Theodore Roethke*; and for excerpts from *Technicians of the Sacred* edited by Jerome Rothenberg, copyright ©1968 by Jerome Rothenberg. Harper & Row, for excerpts from *Seven Arrows* by Hyemeyohsts Storm, copyright ©1972 by Hyemeyohsts Storm. New Directions Publishing Corporation, for an excerpt from *Paterson* by William Carlos Williams, copyright ©1948 by William Carlos Williams. Sierra Club Books, for an excerpt from *The Unsettling of America* by Wendell Berry, copyright ©1977 by Wendell Berry. *The Pacific Sun*, for excerpts from "Surviving Vision Quest," by Steven Foster. Natalie Rogers, for excerpts from her book, *Emerging Woman, A Decade of Midlife Transitions*, copyright © by Natalie Rogers. Rites of Passage, Inc., for excerpts from *A Vision Quest Handbook* by Gift Bearer and others, copyright ©1980. Princeton University Press, for an excerpt from *Hero With a Thousand Faces* by Joseph Campbell, Bollingen Series XVII. Copyright 1949 by Princeton University Press. Copyright © renewed 1976 by Princeton University Press. Book 2: Photo by Willie Stapp. Book 3: Photo, upper left by Marilyn Riley.

Published in 1987 by Prentice Hall Press
A Division of Simon & Schuster, Inc.
Gulf + Western Building
One Gulf + Western Plaza
New York, NY 10023

Originally published by Bear Tribe Publishing, Spokane, WA

PRENTICE HALL PRESS is a trademark of Simon & Schuster, Inc.

Foster, Steven, 1938–
    The book of the vision quest.

    Originally published: Covelo, Calif.: Island Press.
    Bibliography: p.
    1. Spiritual life.   2. Rites and ceremonies.
3. Vision quests.   I. Little, Meredith, 1951–
II. Title.
BL624.F67   1987   291.3′8   87-19320
ISBN 0-13-080110-0 (pbk.)

Manufactured in the United States of America

10 9 8 7 6 5 4 3 2 1

First Prentice Hall Press Edition

For M, in memory of
Κιονιον Ιθαχη
and
For Tom Pinkson, in memory of
The Yosemite

Contents

New Preface to the Second Edition

Returning from the Last Chance Mountains with a group of vision questers, we were presented with the news that Prentice Hall Press would accept this new, expanded edition of *The Book of the Vision Quest* for publication. The season is autumn. The leaves of the cottonwoods are turning the bright golden glow of death. It seems entirely appropriate that winter should be almost here.

Soon the dark of the year will come. What will keep the people warm through the long, cold nights when the trees stand bare and the aching wind sows seeds of yearning to the iron earth? Some say the wheels of war will carry us back again to the dark ages. Others say that Armageddon is at hand. Still others, preferring to make no further effort to swim upstream, turn away from the global realities of human survival, and endlessly contemplate themselves in media mirrors that lie, that tell them they will never grow old, that they will never want or suffer, that no matter how they treat her, the Earth will always be technicolor green. Of course, there are always the legions who say, "Follow like sheep and you will escape the slaughter."

Here is our contribution to the survivial of the people through the coming winter. Here is a fire, fueled by human hearts, ignited by dreams of human wholeness. Here is a warm flame from which light may be drawn to illumine the cold hearths of the world.

We have been especially pleased to learn that this book has penetrated the Iron Curtain and found an audience among Soviet citizens who, like Americans, are looking for ways to revive the power of ancient rites of passage within their culture. Requests for the book have also come from Germany, Sweden, the Netherlands, South Africa, Zambia, Mexico, Honduras, New Zealand, Australia, the United Kingdom, and so on. The interest of diverse people sug-gests the relevance of rites of passage such as the vision quest to diverse cultures. This relevance is not surprising. The archetype is a prominent feature of the human collective unconscious.

For this edition we are especially grateful for the help of Marlise Wabun James Wind, Sun Bear, the Bear Tribe, Bill Thompson, and the copy and graphics editors of Prentice Hall Press. Power to the people.

Steven Foster
Meredith Little
The School of Lost Borders
Big Pine, California
1987

Preface to the First Edition

This book is about the re-creation, in modern times, of an ancient rite of dying, passing through, and being reborn. It is also the story of the efforts of a small nonprofit corporation called Rites of Passage, Inc. (Novato, California), to assist urban and suburban people to go into the wilderness to enact this ancient rite of passage: the Vision Quest.

This book is the first of its kind. It speaks with a collective voice and a single voice. It speaks not only from the local universe of individuals, but from the common universe in which we all live, and in which we have lived since time began. The words are in the English language, but the expression is pan-human.

The Vision Quest experience of which these voices speak is the indirect outgrowth of teaching methods that I began to practice as an Assistant Professor in the School of Humanities at San Francisco State University during the tumultuous years of 1969–1971. Research into American mythology led me to the rites of passage of the first people of America. Other research into the roots of mythology led me to various other rites of initiation, some of them ancient, others not so ancient.

Idealistically, I envisioned a school that would perform a *maieutic* function, acting Socratically, as a midwife, to prepare people in transition to enact a personally meaningful, symbolic act or rite of passage within a natural context. This context, this wilderness womb, would provide nourishment, learning and preparation for reentry into the stream of human time, lending to each student a personal mythic mission to give away.

However, the channels through which such concepts could be taught did not exist within the institutional framework. I was baffled and frustrated by seemingly insurmountable obstacles. When I left college teaching, I swore I would never go back to it.

At that point I went into the desert on my own search. I was stimulated by the recent appearance of a strange and powerful new book, the magic of a modern Native American shield maker, a chief—Hyemeyohsts Storm's *Seven Arrows*. This man wrote, in clear, urgent words: "The Vision Quest, or perceiving quest, is the way we must begin this search. We must all follow our Vision Quest to discover ourselves, to learn how we perceive of ourselves, and to find our relationship with the world around us."

When I returned from the desert I was lost for a while. Finally, one rainy day, I found a man—or he found me. His name was Edward L. Beggs and he was the director of a federally-funded adolescent drug abuse family service agency known as (like a bolt of lightning!) Rites of Passage.

I remember the day well. I had met Edward at a meeting, and afterward we walked back to our cars together and talked. Our talk continued absurdly in the rain for an hour or so, while I shivered from excitement and the cold. Later, in 1973, I went to work for Edward (and the "Feds") at Rites of Passage, which in those days offered a variety of services to young people: therapy, counseling, education in the meaning of rites of passage, even a sex-information hot-line. Much went on in the name of treatment for drug abuse that was not specifically such. For three years I was paid for doing something different from what my job description prescribed.

It was at Rites of Passage that the Vision Quest, as it now exists, first began to take form. It could not have existed without the encouragement of Edward Beggs. Others appeared also: Tom Pinkson and Vern Muhr, the director and instructor of the Marin Open House Wilderness Project. This project, conceived by Tom to help rehabilitate junkies and speed-freaks, was imaginative and courageous. Before long, an exchange of ideas and enthusiasm resulted in the creation of a Vision Quest wilderness ritual, a rite of passage.

In 1974 I went to the Tiltill Valley of the Yosemite with a dozen other people to reenact seriously what we thought was the first Vision Quest of recent white European history. This act culminated three years of seeking my own vision amid the despair and frustrations of my own life and the lives of many I lived with. I was volunteering at Suicide Prevention at the time and seeking some way to quell my deepest fears that I had nothing worthwhile to give away. I could not have known that I had actually completed a passage and that my ship had landed on the shore of a new world. Nor could I have known that my Suicide Prevention "shift partner" would become my wife and work partner two years later.

Before my stay in the original Rites of Passage was terminated, I had participated in a dozen Vision Quests, mainly involving young people on the verge of leaving home. The more involved with the concept I became, the more convinced I was that the vision for my life lay there, with the teaching of rites of passage and the reintroduction of ancient birth-ways into the desert of meaninglessness that is modern American culture.

But the "Feds" said no. They decided, somewhere in the dim halls of NIDA, that funds were being misappropriated on such things as Vision Quests. In June of 1976 Rites of Passage ceased to be, and I was footloose with my myth, with no cultural socket to plug it into.

For a year I let the vision go. I was in love with Meredith, Lonely Heart Outreaching. We went to Europe and then to Greece, to a tiny village on the island of Ithaki, home of Odysseus, the wide-wanderer. Amid the romance and simple reality of life on Ithaki I almost forgot the Vision Quest. My love and I walked in the moonlight above the ancient village of Annoghi and, drawn by the dark and fertile sea, decided to make a baby.

Only then, when Meredith was pregnant with Selene, did we begin to face the dare that lurked in our homeland, in our old neighborhood, in our hearts. As the vision grew again with a new urgency between the two of us, we began to feel the increasing tension between our Greek home and our Marin County home. We made plans to return and take up the Vision Quest work.

But how? We had just enough money to fly back and rent a house for a month. Meredith was looking like a pear. It was probably not the best time to set out on the trail of a star. We returned to America from our island of myth, certain about what we sought, uncertain about the means to go about it.

Then the little miracles began to occur: a little money here, a donation there, the discovery that people were willing to pay us to prepare them for the Vision Quest. Edward Beggs, now living in Tennessee, agreed to relinquish his rights to the use of the name, Rites of Passage, for our nonprofit corporation. His beautiful gift was followed by powerful encouragement and support from Dr. Tom Pinkson, the man with whom I had originally conceived of the Vision

Quest ritual and who had become involved in similar work at the College of Marin. Tom has since shifted his visionary energy to people who face life's greatest Vision Quest: death itself. He has become a spiritual ally to us.

Rites of Passage, Inc., was incorporated as a nonprofit, charitable, educational corporation in September, 1977. Since then, Meredith and I have accompanied over thirty different groups into the wilderness of the Great Basin, groups composed of young people and/or adults—our neighbors, the people of our shire, people who are challenged to seek a vision in an ancient yet modern manner. It has not always been easy or fun. It has been difficult to convince foundations and educational institutions that living alone, fasting, and crying for a vision in the wilderness can be beneficial and healthful, even though the idea has been around for a long time and sparkles in the lives of many of our religious saints and heroes.

Many friends have come to help. Some have helped materially, others spiritually. Some, like Gift Bearer, have helped in both ways. Some of those who first came are gone now. Others have stayed. New allies arrive. Constant through it all has been the presence of Lonely Heart Outreaching. Because we dared to believe that the love between us was God, we were freed to know that *the* vision was *our* vision. Without her, the book would not have been written. The rigors of the quest have led us through the Slough of Despond to the ramparts of the Castle of Despair, but she has borne herself calmly, rationally on.

Her tireless work (typing, preparing the manuscript, reading and selecting from journals) has kept steady pace with the evolution of the concept behind the book. Again and again she freed me from my usual duties with our family of five, so that I could apply the seat of my pants to the solitude required to finish the manuscript. I love her more than this book can say.

A man who at the age of seventeen participated in that first Yosemite Vision Quest, a poet named Silence, came to work with us a year ago and remains to this day, a trained midwife for people who want to birth themselves through the Vision Quest. A strong, smiling, ever-deepening young man with a fire in his heart, he is teaching me how to say thank you.

More recently, Gift Bearer and Looking Into the Fire have come each with their intelligence, energy, beauty and unique gifts to further the Vision

Quest work and to encourage the fruition of the book. Looking Into the Fire has brought charisma, determination and leadership to a role she never imagined she would play. Within her heart she carries the knowledge of the regenerative power of a rite of passage.

Gift Bearer brings her training, her intelligence, her shamanistic and pedagogical genius. Her work as an anthropologist and a writer has consistently challenged and enriched the basic premises of this effort. She is the source of much of the form and meaning of Book 2.

Other people throng to be mentioned, people who, for one reason or another, have been as the salt of the earth to this book: Derham Giuliani, Louise Malfanti, Dreams a Lot (Tim Garthwaite), Eye in the Star (Char Hornig), Philip and Elizabeth Little, Tree Strong and Nourishing (Ron Peavny), Barbara Dean, Strong Tree (Jan Duncan), Sam Wilcox, Pat Nalley, George Rideout, Del Rio, Georgia Oliva, Little Warrior (Steve DeMartini), Marv and Marilyn of Desert Mountain Rescue, my mother and father, and many others.

Nor should I neglect to mention a man whom I know as Rolling Thunder on the Mountain, of Thunder Mountain, Nevada, who pointed up to the steep ridges of Thunder Mountain and said: "See up there? Two canyons. One is Sacred Canyon and the other is Thunder Canyon. Go up there, and don't come back until the voices have stopped."

Steven Foster
(Heart In His Throat)
Forgotten Creek
Death Valley

This is the dead land.
This is the cactus land.
Here the stone images
Are raised, here they receive
The supplication of a dead man's hand
Under the twinkle of a fading star.

Is it like this
In death's other kingdom
Walking alone
At the hour when we are
Trembling with tenderness.
Lips that would kiss
Form prayers to broken stone.
—T. S. Eliot, "The Hollow Men"

BOOK 1

1. THE QUEST

What can be known? The unknown.
My true self runs toward a Hill.
More! O More! visible.

Now I adore my life
With the Bird, the abiding Leaf,
With the Fish, the questing Snail,
And the Eye altering all;
And I dance with William Blake
For love, for Love's sake . . . .

—Theodore Roethke, "Once More, The Round"

Many years ago, haunted by guilt, pursued by images of freedom, persistently, relentlessly believing that I had to acquire experience at the risk of all, I left my vocation of college teaching and went into the world. Though I lived with great appetite, and seemed, even to myself, suicidally bent on my own destruction or the destruction of anyone who loved me, I found myself drawn into the land of my father's childhood and early manhood: the vast stretches of loneliness called Nevada, and the remote, desolate regions of the desert called Mojave.

I went into the desert alone, not knowing why, searching for something

I had lost, or would find: something, someone, some revelation waiting for me at the bend of the dry river bed, some face to face encounter with what I feared, and desired, most.

At the time I did not realize I was seeking death. That is, I was not seeking to die, but to reap the fruit of death, to reenter the womb of things, the matrix of unknowing, and to be born anew, severed from old distinctions and limitations, to induce, by sheer force of will, self-transformation.

But self-transformation is a gradual, painstaking process won at the expense of joy and sorrow, or so it has been for me. Nevertheless, certain power-events, or growth-events, blaze out from the background of my life. These events mark the juncture at which my restless, seeking heart touched the structureless, timeless, transforming heart of the universe. The year I spent in the desert was filled with many such events.

Was it because my mother told me I had been conceived at Shadow Mountain, within view of the mountains of Death Valley, that I went into the desert? Was it because my childhood had been steeped in the stories of the Old Testament, the tales of the desert prophets, Moses, Isaiah, Elijah? Was it because, even when I was very small, I felt a deep affinity with the spirit of the desert? Something lured me. I responded with instinctive faith in a feeling that quickened me to the core, a shuddering, shivering, passionate feeling.

I packed an old VW bus with a few essentials, said goodbye to my children, my friends and my life, and drove away. I headed east toward Reno, gateway to the far-flung deserts of the Great Basin. I came back, eventually, to pick up the threads of my "civilized" life, a life that had changed because I had changed.

But when I got into my car and took off down the road, I gave no thought to returning. I had reached a point where desperation overshadowed responsibilities. I could not continue living as I had been living. Something more was waiting. Surely, if I actively sought it, the answer would be revealed to me out there, in the trackless waste. I drove away with such deep excite-ment. I had not thought I was capable of such emotion.

What happened to me in the desert? I cannot exactly say. I am con-vinced that the Great Mother eventually led me to heights and depths of being that are akin to what the prophets called vision or *God*. I was not prepared to understand all that came to pass. Much of the time I was dealing with my own ignorance and the basic questions of my survival.

Though for years I had made pronouncements about the nature of life to students from my ivory tower, I knew very little about the face of our Great Mother. The night I left the last town and turned my face to the wilderness I realized how inadequately I had prepared myself. I trembled with fear and considered going back. What if I died out there? It might be a long time before somebody found me. What if I got lost? I would have nowhere to go, no one to come home to, to help me find myself. I feared insanity. I feared flash floods, rattlesnakes, the dark, the cold, bad roads, car trouble, dying of thirst. Most of all, I feared loneliness. All my heroic myths about myself came down like the walls of Jericho when I first heard, really heard, the awesome trumpet sound of the loneliness of the wilderness – the sound of *silence*. Against that I was nothing but a cipher. My ego withered, as pages of a book thrown to a fire.

How little I knew about survival, or myself, or death. Having rejected all other teachings, I had apprenticed myself to the most exacting teacher of all. But I did not understand her language. Her voice was the roaring of silence in my ears. She taught, not with words, but through my body, with light and darkness, rain and wind, snow and fire. And the words she caused me to utter were not the words of the world I knew. Some of them were cries that came from my stomach and bowels, strange to my ears, more like those of an animal: howls, moans, grunts and growls. And the actions she taught me were animal actions, almost forgotten: eating, sleeping, eliminating, creeping, burrowing, hiding, being alert even when asleep. The learning of these gestures marked the beginnings of change in my life.

Is it the vulnerability of loneliness that drives us to love and to be loved? The implacable stars and the horned moon ride the night sky, leaving the ache and emptiness of another morning without love in their wake. Thus we learn to live with loneliness, to curse and accept it, to fill it with the rituals of survival. But finally loneliness would break me down into rigid insistence: my body *craved,* as dry leaves crave the wind, the presence of another. I would go into Winnemucca or Austin or Goldfield or Darwin or Benton Springs, looking for someone to talk to.

In a way, loneliness is death, or a form of death. Once, as I drove a long, desolate stretch of highway between Wells and Ely, I overtook a young woman walking down the road, without pack or water, twenty-five miles north of Currie. Imagining she was in trouble or needed a lift, I stopped and asked her if I could be of help.

She looked at me from a face blistered by the sun. She saw a wild-looking man, dirty, unshaven, horizons gleaming in his eyes. I saw a weary woman with a wasted longing in her eyes.

"No thanks," she said.

Curious, I asked her what she was doing here, out in the middle of nowhere.

"Nowhere is somewhere," she replied curtly and kept on walking.

So I drove on. Her toiling form shrank in the rear view mirror, until she was just a speck, which then vanished. I sometimes wonder about her. She reminded me of myself. Surely she was one of those lonely, lost people learning how to die.

Many a night I spent watching unidentified lights move on the horizon. Sometimes they appeared to approach. This optical phenomenon so frightened me one night that I sat up all night by the fire, reluctant to close my eyes in sleep against the possible unknown terror the moving lights represented. Many a night I spent frightened, uncomfortable, anxious, restless, in a vague dread that calamity would befall me. Many a night I lay awake, remembering my children, my women, my family, my friends. Many a morning I awoke to the bitter taste of emptiness in my coffee, and for several days the pangs of unrequited love would keep me from food. Spasms of self-pity would come and go. Sometimes I heard the strange sound of a man crying for himself.

One early summer day in Dry Lake Valley, west of Caliente, Nevada, surely one of the most desolate regions of the earth, I ingested enough LSD for a dozen people. Reasoning that if I was to seize the fire from the altar, this was the way to do it, I entered the morning with high expectations. By noon the temperature had risen to intolerable limits, and I had no shelter but my car, which had become a furnace. At 4:00 p.m. I got into the car and drove all the way to Lake Mead and camped that night in the Valley of Fire. What had occurred had not been in the nature of a revelation. I had walked several miles along a bad jeep road that only led me deeper into burning, infernal regions. A lizard slipped across my path, and I jumped a county mile. I wrote in my journal some time during the day: "If I am God, then why is God afraid of his own shadow?" I was badly sunburned and in some pain through the night. The next day God drove into Las Vegas and bought a hamburger and a chocolate malt, never to drop LSD again.

Nevertheless, I persisted in believing that eventually I would attain a vision. I sought places in the earth that were haunted by the ghosts of Native American souls, isolated springs and mountain tops, canyons crawling with rattlesnakes and cats, stone quarries where percussion flakes of obsidian, agate and chert lay on the ground like snow unmelted for hundreds of years. I drank from the creeks of the Toiyabes and the Inyos, slept in the arroyos of the Funerals and the Paradise, climbed the ridges of the Black, Ruby, and Last Chance. Everywhere my teacher surrounded me with beauty and terror. She assailed my senses with the smell of sage, the taste of native trout, the scatter and gather of little birds. The coyote chilled me with calls that imitated the crying of my children. The rattlesnake hissed from the damp reeds. The half-rotted carcass of a burro grinned up at me from Crystal Spring.

I became aware that Nature spoke to me when I emptied my ears of my own internal dialogue. I saw many powerful teachings, when my eyes were not distracted by my brain. I prepared my heart through fasting and attention to detail, watching by the hour as the leaves of cottonwoods collected the solar wind. I thought every now and then about dying.

Many strange and wonderful instances of the Great Mother's creation were revealed to me. But I never had a vision, if by "vision" is meant that which is perceived by other than mortal sight. When the time came to return to civilization, the same man returned who went forth. Nature, his teacher, had worked profound alterations in his heart, but he was the same man.

I knew more about this soul-system, this cocoon. I knew I was an eye with two blind feet. My emptiness craved motion; my fire craved fuel; my ears craved the music of silence; my arms craved the rough, red earth; my feet craved miles; my thirst craved more deeply than any desert spring could satisfy. "Who are you?" the unshielded sun roared at me, tearing away the letters of my name from the being who crouched inside. The sun made me write a poem about him, tear it out of my journal, and fling it on the wasteland

21

for the scorpion to read. He made me know myself then.

The desert, my Mother, taught me that the flash of a mockingbird's wing is more precious than the finest sapphire. She taught me that the smell of wet sage is more lush than any poet's words. Through her I came to know my belly when it was hungry, my eyes when they were wide open, my voice when it was choked by my heart, my ears when they were dirty, my genitals when they were forgotten, my breast when emptied of loneliness by loneliness, my legs when they were called on for another mile.

Above all, I learned that my way would be hard, that my way would require courage, endurance, independence and all the wits I possessed, that my way was narrow, dangerous, precise, spiraling ever upward, skirting the edge, threading the shuttle of my heart between the warp and woof of life and death. I learned that it did not matter what others thought so long as I kept to the inner path which led to the final, ecstatic assimilation of contradiction in death; that my path was lonely, that death walked with me — he the body, I the shadow — into high noon. I learned to submit to my mortality, but never to my death.

The decision to return to civilization came suddenly one afternoon while I was in the laundromat in Elko, Nevada, the town where my quest had begun. It occurred to me, as I watched the locals and tourists do what I was doing, that I was not truly afraid of being alone anymore. In fact, I preferred it. My real problem was that I was afraid of being with people.

All at once I remembered my children. The life I had exiled myself from crashed in on me. I was overwhelmed by the reality of my situation. Aside from being a hermit, I really did not know what to do with my life. I was nearing middle age; my children were scattered; I had no mate; I had no money; I had no home.

I did have a civilized name: Steven Foster. The making of the sound of it was foreign in my mouth. The idea that the name was connected to the being who had been wandering the earth, scouring his body with sun and moon and wind, was confusing and disheartening. I wanted to remain with my spiritual ancestors, the Paiute, and dance the Ghost Dance. I gave myself a name: Heart in His Throat.

As my clothes whirled in the dryer, I went over all the old contradictions between Nature and civilization. Never did I abhor the latter more. But my heart, which I had come to respect, said calmly: "Go back to your life and your loved ones. Work it out there. That which you fear most is the source of ultimate revelation and power. Go and learn to live with people."

So I went back to live a life I was reluctant to lead, to take my place as a man in the adult world of Marin County, California. I went back to live alone, as a single male and a divorced father. It was shaky at first. It was difficult to imprison my shadow under roofs and artificial lights. I feared humans, the most dangerous of animals. I feared my own social reactions. I was self-conscious and deeply scornful of people who lived artificial lives.

Slowly the freeways claimed me. The beat of the clock parceled out my days. There was somewhere to get to, someone to see and feel emotional about, something to do or something that ought to be done. There were dollars to earn and an infinite number of places to spend them. Gradually, the memory of my desert life retreated, attenuated by the insistent need to survive in the wilderness of the city. I forgot to practice the lessons my Teacher had imparted: the lessons of patience, fortitude, clear sight and animal ease. I began to question the relevance of my wilderness education to the practical necessities of survival in a wilderness more savage than any desert.

The mother of my children needed money and my children needed their father. The rent had to be paid, the master cylinder replaced, the check-out stand to be endured, the feet to be well-heeled, the body made respectable with clothing. This seemed no dark night of the soul I faced; this was an endless round of pseudo-events, a whirl of arbitrary deadlines. For a long while my heart of hearts would not accept the idea that money had anything to do with survival. When I finally had to accept this fact, I accepted it bitterly.

Yet it *was* a dark night of the soul I had descended into. The impregnating joys of the wilderness were gone. The sorrows of bringing forth had commenced. I was not to be granted the privilege of being taught by the Great Mother without the responsibility of carrying these teachings to others. For a long time I resented the burden. But the vision of my life began to grow, regardless, in the close, anxious darkness of despair.

Something was being born in me. The tenseness and dismay of my life were due to labor pains developing in the region of my heart and pushing upward into an aching void in my throat. My days were the placenta upon which fed the roots and tendrils of an unenvisioned dream. The uterine dream, call it a dream of destiny, kicked and stretched in the bland plasma of unuttered words and silently mouthed.

As with any birth, death precedes release. I had to die before my mind could read the words reflected on the mirror of my heart. Exactly when I died I do not remember. It might have been one rainy afternoon I walked out to the mailbox, only to find it empty again. The actual time of death does not matter. What does matter was the fact that in dying I had to let go of the old ways of seeing myself and place my faith in the unknown.

I also had to let go of the desert, to let her go knowing that her mountains would always be there, exposed and impassive, waiting for me to impregnate her with my human consciousness. If ever I was to regain her, fully and totally, as a man of heart, I must leave her to herself and cling to my birthing vision. If the trail of my heart led me deeper into the greedy stomach of the monster of civilization, then I would go. I would allow myself to be swallowed up, but only so as to discover how to cut my way out. I was not helpless. I was not without abilities. I could learn to love. I could learn to teach again. I could save myself.

I determined, therefore, to put in some time volunteering on the Marin County Suicide Prevention Hotline. I did so not because I believed it was immoral to commit suicide, but because my heart tugged me to it. A friend had taken the time to suggest that I might benefit from doing such work. The idea appealed to me. I could cast my voice into the wasteland and from my loneliness touch another human soul with the gift of the heart in my throat.

I enrolled in Suicide Prevention training and was ultimately introduced to the first symbol of my birthing vision—the Hotline Room. It was in this room with the telephones, the red light and the big log book, that the temper of my heart was tested, as though by fire. It was in this room, late at night or early in the morning, rubbing the weariness from my brain, that I learned to listen to the despairing voices of lonely people and the tragedy of their lives.

The Hotline Room was the despair center of the city. Into it poured the electrical impulses of the disembodied voices of lonely human souls in crisis. The telephone, like a synapse, plugged live voices into each other and

24

catalyzed a human drama of love and despair. The Hotline Room was a big ear. It listened to the stories that were secret and hidden, stories about the darkness and the other side of things, stories of people who were dying.

But the ear had a voice and a myth. The voice was like a lighthouse beacon, a heartbeat, the regular, steady breath of a living organism. It sent out the reassuring myth: "We are all lonely. But life is good; it is worthwhile living it. Be here when tomorrow comes. Someday you will find love." I did not always personally believe in this myth. Many times I would rather have said, "Go ahead and get it over with. Die and be happy." It seemed absurd to me that suicide should be unlawful. I was not always able to love those who called, or believe that, given the difficulties they faced, they would ever find love. But there were others who challenged me to help them to see for themselves that their life was, indeed, worth living. Many reminded me of myself. I trembled inside when I talked to them. I was learning how to love.

The Hotline Room taught me many things. It taught me that hate was not the only enemy of love. So also were guilt and anger and self-pity and hypocrisy and greed and indifference and deceit and many other things. Love seemed to have more enemies than any other truth. And yet it seemed to be stronger even than death. The Hotline Room taught me to listen, to weigh, to be fair, and to be patient, and yet it created an urgency in me to go deeper into this matter of loneliness, to venture another day into this wilderness of pain and sorrow and confront the monster in his lair.

One night I called Suicide Prevention myself, just to see what it felt like to be a caller. I made up a fictitious name and played myself a few years before. I knew the part well. The person who spoke to me was tired, but he was patient and loving with me. He said, "If you're ever down again, give me a call." Did he really mean it? I think so.

Doubtless, all those who called had one thing in common: they were lonely. Living with a wife or husband in a crowded apartment building, they were lonely. The gynecologist, fearful that he was gay, was lonely. John Doe, fading out on an undisclosed number of Valium, was lonely. The eleven-year-old girl lying in bed with multiple fractures and no mother or father, was lonely. Josh, lying naked on the floor of his apartment, drunk as a skunk, cradling a shotgun in his arms, was lonely. Jane Doe, having awakened from two days of semi-consciousness following a beating by her boyfriend, was lonely. The housewife, calling to say she was afraid she was battering her children, was lonely. The overweight young woman pretending to be talked out of dropping a dozen reds, who hung up and dropped them anyway, was lonely.

In the morning when the shift was over, I would walk into the streets of Marin County, looking into eyes. I would want to stop certain people and say, "Weren't you the one who called Suicide Prevention last night and told me you were dying of leukemia and that your boyfriend was getting interested in someone else?" But by the light of day all seemed changed and new. Another day had dawned. It was time to start afresh. I prayed that all those people who had called me the night before would have their miracles today. But loneliness had come to dwell in the city and to stalk the night streets. Next time I came on shift, the voices called again: "No, I don't have any friends. I'm fat and ugly. People think I'm crazy but I'm not. They just don't like me."

Many a night I had to drag myself to the Hotline Room, unwilling to face the challenge of yet another night of it. What was it that drew me? I was fascinated and frightened by the emotion of loneliness. It seemed to me that God lived there in its cruel depths, that loneliness somehow was the soil in which sprouted the seeds of love.

"Loneliness is the teacher of giving," says Hyemeyohsts Storm. Every time I picked up the phone there was a touching, a giving. As I came to recognize this bridging of unknowing between two souls, I began to see. I began to see what I could do, as a man, in this world where belief and myth seem to have broken down into passivity and cynicism.

The vision first took form as a decision to love people, that is, to care consciously about their loneliness, to care whether they died lonely and out of balance, to care about the fact that we were all out of balance and in imminent danger of self-annihilation. Later, as I became more relaxed and maneuverable within the driving force of that vision, I realized it was the *only* thing I could do, and I would do it because doing it meant I was on the trail. Even in times of great weariness and despair, on the trail, I would go to sleep and die, only to rise the next morning born anew, ready to get back on my feet and on the way.

I got myself back up because the desolate winds of the wilderness still stirred the wildflowers growing in the springtime of my heart. Though I had let the Great Mother go from the press and demand of city life, she was always with me. She continued to speak to me through rain and sun, through a patch of weeds in a back alley. She renewed me, challenged me to see my neighbors as manifestations of myself. She challenged me to look into open wounds, into the wounds humanity had made on her body. She challenged me to consider how I might be a channel through whom she might heal these wounds. It was she who spoke into the telephone, when I could let her, into the ears of the loneliness that called.

And so the vision came from my heart, where tears of joy and sorrow are born in the throat and hammered by language into words. The vision of my life was this:

I saw the distant peaks and barren ridges of a desert land. Above a nameless canyon, a raven cut out from the night shadow of death coiled in the wind. In the canyon below was a man, his shoulder hunched against a great, unmoving wall of stone, his tin cup filling with a faint seeping trickle of cool spring water. In such a wild, thirsty land he might have been any man, seeking to stay alive. He happened to be me.

I was in this desert place because my people and I were thirsty and had nothing to drink. I knew where this spring was, deep in the rock-bound desert, and had gone there to spoon the precious gift of life into my water jugs. But I had to work quickly, for night was falling, and I would not be able to find my way back to the others in the dark.

I saw that the desert land and the nameless canyon with its tiny seep was my heart. I saw that the water I collected in my jug were tears oozing from my heart. These tears, pure and from the Source of Life, came up from me because I was crying inwardly. Why was I crying? Because I had been given the opportunity by the Great Mother to find water and bring it back to the others, to be a water bearer.

I saw that my journey would be an inward one, into the wilderness of my heart, and a double-edged outward journey, into the wilderness of rock, sand and water, and into the wild, tangled jungle of other people's lives. These wildernesses, so dissimilar, yet of the same source, were bridged, connected and made one, when I drew water from the rock.

It was then that I began to conceive of a means by which I could share this vision with others on a more personal level than through Suicide Prevention. I had learned, through many a long night, that many of my neighbors were on the threshold, as I had been. Among these people the Vision Quest was created, first as a concept yearning to be born, and finally as actual practice.

In the beginning there were few who cared or understood. But these few counted for a great deal. We came together finally to enact for the first time the rite of passage we called the Vision Quest. It was late spring in Yosemite. It was not my beloved desert. Everything was a riot of green. I found a glacial boulder from which gushed a tiny waterfall. Beside that waterfall, for three days and nights, I fasted and cried for a vision. The waterfall spoke to me. This is what it said: You must look within your heart and see what you have to give to your people. Then you must go back and give it away. I looked within and saw what I had to give away.

When I left everything behind and went into the wilderness, I did what people have done for generations in countless cultures. The process and the truth of the process are profoundly connected to the collective unconscious, of which I was but a discrete member. The force of all those who had gone before entered me, not because I was worthy, but because I was human.

This vision is not *my* vision. It is *our* vision. In a greater sense it is a vision from the heart of the Great Mother, the same heart that in ancient times spoke from within human beings of many lands and origins, including the original Asian people of America. And all of us who have followed this vision have entered a suspended time, an archetypal river of collective, unconscious knowing, a time of being alone with the Great Mother. The vision has helped us to grow, to change ourselves, to transform our lives with myth. Above all, the vision helped us to learn to love, respect and cherish each other, to walk in balance between the two worlds, to Giveaway, to worship the fire in the heart of the Great Mother who brought us into being.

BOOK 2

2. The Ritual

I received a letter containing an account of a recent suicide:

"My friend . . . jumped off the Golden Gate Bridge two months ago. She had been terribly depressed for years. There was no help for her. None that she could find that was sufficient. She was trying to get from one phase of her life to another, and couldn't make it. She had been terribly wounded as a child. . . . Her wound could not be healed. She destroyed herself."

The letter had already asked, "How does a human pass through youth to maturity without breaking down?" And it had answered, "help from tradition, through ceremonies and rituals, rites of passage at the most difficult stages."
—Wendell Berry, The Unsettling of America

Imagine that you have decided to experience a Vision Quest. You must know from the beginning that the Vision Quest is a rite of passage. A rite of passage is an experience by which an individual or a group formally expresses the attainment of a new life status, a symbolic experience of dying and being born into a new way.

In early times, among more traditional or primitive cultures, the transitions of life were clearly defined. Birth, childhood, adulthood, marriage, old age and death were formalized with rites of passage. In modern culture, life transitions are not so clearly defined; our modern life has been demythologized. In the process of becoming technically advanced, modern culture has lost its traditional ways of perpetuating itself through ritual and meaningful, formal growth events. But in casting aside these ancient, proven ways of marking transition, we have impoverished our lives. There is a basic hunger that cannot be satisfied by material abundance alone.

Nowadays, a life transition is not seen in terms of a single, decisive, transformational event by which new status is attained. We often stumble through our adolescence, our marriages, our separations and divorces, our geographical uprootings, our life-threatening illnesses, our bereavements and our retirements, ill-prepared to experience and understand them. We fail to notice that by our experience we evolve discretely, stage by stage, with many little deaths and rebirths.

A rite of passage is the traditional cultural answer to a personal crisis of meaning. Through the rite of passage, individuals and groups make themselves receptive to spiritual meaning. Contact with this spiritual meaning (God, The Great Spirit, the Life Force, higher consciousness) resolves the crisis, and the transition is accomplished.

The Vision Quest that you have decided to experience has been drawn from the past. It is a primitive rite of passage adapted to meet the needs of people who live in a modern culture. It is structured to draw upon the power of ancient archetype and symbol, but only to provide you with tools for the spontaneous creation of your own myths, your own rituals, replete with your own meanings. Only the bare bones, the structural skeleton underlying all such rituals, are made available to you.

Certain basic themes or phases common to all rites of transition were identified by Arnold van Gennep in the classic *Les rites de passage*. These three phases can be likened to an opening of the door, a stepping across the threshold, and a returning through the door from the other side.

The first phase is *severance,* or separation from the parents, the home, the family, the context of daily life, the world of human responsibility, privileges, and "the clock"—separation from the temporal world. The individual is required to leave it all behind, to consider the former life to be at an end. The individual is taken away to a place apart and prepares to undergo the second phase of the rite of passage.

The second phase is called *liminal* (Latin: "threshold"). It entails the direct, existential experience of the meaning of a life transition. The partici-pant steps across the threshold into the unknown, armed with symbolic tools of self-birth, and enters a universal order that is sacred and immortal. During this threshold period, secret knowledge and power are transmitted and confer on the individual new rights, privileges and responsibilities upon returning.

The third phase, *reincorporation,* involves the return of the seeker from the spiritual realm of power and knowing to the mortal realm of civilization and the community. Ideally, the individual is culturally supported in living out externally the internal changes that have taken place during the rite of passage.

This three-phase dynamic—severance, threshold, and reincorporation— is the basic structure of the Vision Quest. This same process might be seen as a metaphor for the dynamic of life itself: severance from the mother at birth, immersion in the threshold experiencing of life, and reincorporation into the Great Mother at death. Going forth, being, returning. Imagine a wave, breaking in, pausing, and returning to the ocean. Note that the wave, upon returning to the community, carries with it a residue, a part of the sacred shore.

Severance

*Nothing can be sole or whole that has not
been rent.*
*— W. B. Yeats, "Crazy Jane Talks With
the Bishop"*

First you must prepare yourself to sever. You will be required to attend a
series of classes where you will meet with others who have decided to experience the Vision Quest. You will learn pertinent survival information, including
emergency field procedures. You will study Native American and other
archaic rites of passage. You will talk about your life, your own deaths and
rebirths. You will talk about your own life-myths and their relationship to
your behavior. You will talk about the world you are preparing to leave behind
and the world that you are coming back to. After a while, you will begin to
feel the sense of shared group commitment that binds groups together in
community and love.

    The time will come when you load your pack and climb into the bus
that will take you to the wilderness. You will be there for about six days,
three of which you will spend living alone, fasting and seeking a vision. The
long journey to the wilderness will sever you from the context of your normal
life and set you face to face with the mirror of your evolutionary roots.
Whether you are at a turning point in your life cycle or merely in need of
renewal to maintain a chosen path, you are going back to the wellspring from
which humankind has always drawn its spiritual wisdom and strength – the
mothering earth. You are following a universal orientation toward the physical
environment widely expressed in myth and ritual from all cultures of all times.

    Those who go with you as "leaders" are not, in fact, leaders at all. They
are midwives. They will accompany you up to the last step of the severance
process; but then they will leave you to face the threshold alone. They will
give you over to yourself. Having brought you thus far, they will recede for
three days and nights into your memory of the world you have left behind.

All rites of passage involve some sort of hardship, risk or trial. As the time for the threshold experience comes closer you may experience some anxiety, expecially if you have never been in the wilderness before, nor slept on the hard ground. Such anxiety is common among experienced sailors and wilderness explorers. Nature is unpredictable. There is always an element of risk, and there is always some fear. The fear can be a slight sensation of nervousness at the pit of the stomach or a full-blown panic. Risk and fear are the Earth Mother's handmaidens. They strip one of pride, rip off the habitual blinders, awaken the sleeping senses. They stir up the capacity to innovate, to create new ways of seeing old situations.

Accept the nervousness and fear. The greater the perceived risk the greater the potential for personal growth, and the more lasting the effects of the experience. Even as you begin preparation for the journey, begin preparation to return. You are severing only because you are returning, no longer connected as before.

Though you will walk as nakedly as possible to your rendezvous with the Great Mother, you must carry some of the tools of civilization. We cannot recapture the early peoples' fine tuning to Nature. We can only simplify the elaborate technological barrier behind which we live our passive, helpless lives.

As you collect your gear in readiness for the trip, you will face many minor choices about what to bring and what to leave behind. This process itself is part of the experience of severance, of sorting out what *for you* is an essential bit of material environment and what you dare to let go of for this brief time. Your fully loaded backpack is symbolic of your attachment to the life you are leaving. The weight of your backpack is like the weight of your karma. Do you really want to carry that much? Like the burden of fear, it may prevent you from getting to where you want to go.

EQUIPMENT

Part of the Vision Quest experience is learning what you can get along without, psychologically and physically. Recognize that as you prepare, you are involved in a symbolic act. You are selecting from your past those things that will make it possible for you to walk into your future. You are finding the delicate balance between the security of the past and the risk of freedom.

Equipment List

backpack	bandanna
sleeping bag	water (2 gallons if a source is not available)
sleeping pad (optional)	journal and pencil
ground cloth or rain tarp	toilet paper
50 feet of rope	warm clothes, stout boots and wool cap
clasp knife	cup and spoon
matches	change of warm clothes

You might want to add other items to this basic list. Some people bring a whole arsenal of goods and services, only to discover no mosquitoes for repellent to repel, nor any fish for pole to snare. Some people want to bring a musical instrument. Only you know what modes of self-expression will enrich your experience. If you want to bring it, you've got to carry it. Radios and tape recorders are not allowed. Music has its place in the wilderness, but the Vision Quest requires music that comes either from you or from the Great Mother.

The journal is not an option. It is a must. You keep it for the sake of your own continued growth, even long after you return.

Food

For three days in the wilderness you will fast. The other days you will eat meals that are shared communally, except for lunches, which are usually eaten when you are away from base camp with a partner. Your contribution to the communal meals will be small, but when everyone shares, everyone is fed. Usually we eat soups and stews full of onions, potatoes, carrots, cheese, cucumber, green pepper, meat (occasionally), and, for the discerning palate, garlic. We put together cabbage quarters, carrots, raw sweet potatoes, turnips, raisins, tuna and hard-boiled eggs and make salads with vinegar and oil dressings. With flour, water, salt and a dash of baking powder, we make flatbread and tortillas. Each member will be expected to do what is necessary to prepare the food and share the kitchen duties. Sharing food, symbolically feeding each other, paying attention to what is being eaten: in such ways the eating of a simple meal in the wilderness becomes a powerful teaching.

Notes to the Neophyte

If you have never worn a backpack before nor slept in a sleeping bag out under the stars, you may be in for a pleasant surprise. To ensure that your surprise is pleasant, test the soundness of your equipment. Your most essential piece of equipment is your body, so now is a good time to start getting in shape. One suggestion is to load your backpack and carry it around on your back. Test its feel against you, upon you. If you have the chance, walk a few miles with your burden. How will it be for you after the first mile? How does your loaded pack fit you? Is the frame too small, too big, too awkward? Can it be adjusted to fit, so that the load is distributed more evenly on your back, or resting more firmly on your hips?

By honestly assessing your abilities and making yourself as ready as you can, you are purifying yourself. Making sure that your equipment is sound and adequate is also a part of the self-purification process.

You might wonder about taking drugs along. Drugs alter perception and thus make it impossible for you to attain utter nakedness of mind. Some drugs are dangerous, especially if you are alone, the nearest person is a mile away, and it is dark. Consult your physician regarding the use of prescription drugs while fasting.

Survival

The wilderness is not a dangerous place. The chances are you will be safer here, even all alone, than in the crowded city. But there are potential hazards, such as those represented by the weather, the terrain, the flora and fauna, and, of course, yourself.

Before you go to the wilderness you must know the symptoms and treatment of heat exhaustion, sunstroke, dehydration, sunburn, exposure, and how they are occasioned and avoided.

Before you go to the wilderness you must have at least a rudimentary conception of the nature and habits of talus slopes, cliffs you can get up but not down, flash floods, thunderstorms, sandstorms and snow. You will need to know how to get yourself out of the wind, how and where and with what to make a fire, and how to go about building a rudimentary shelter and otherwise care for yourself.

37

You will also need to know about the habits of rattlesnakes, scorpions and other stinging insects, and what to do if you are bitten or stung.

You will have a good sense of the parameters of survival within the Vision Quest situation, realizing that, because three days and nights you will be alone, certain emergency procedures and guidelines must be established and adhered to by every member of the group in order to ensure everyone's survival.

THE JOURNEY TO THE WILDERNESS

By night you will travel with the group in a dark passage from the familiar to the new. When the morning light dawns, the world around you will seem strange. Before long the bus will stop. With the others you will put your pack on your back and walk into the wilderness. When you leave the bus, you are leaving the last symbol of home. Cramped as it may have been, at least it had a roof and walls. Now you have entered the sacred theater of Nature.

A few miles away from where you left the bus, the group will establish a base camp. You will orient yourself to the terrain and begin to apply what you have learned.

That night, by the fire, there will be stories and songs. People will talk about their deepest fears, the butterflies they feel in the pit of their stomach. Later, out in the dark, away from the wash of the firelight, tired, cramped bodies will seek unfamiliar sleeping bags. The end of the severance period is near.

The next day, with a buddy who wants to explore in the same direction, you will take a day-long exploratory hike through the canyons and along the ridges, looking for your place. It will feel good to be out in the open, to be stretching your legs, to be poking your nose into nooks and crannies and holes in the ground, to be looking for the place, *your* place, where you will hold communion with Nature. There are few rules about what or where it must be; the finding of it is your affair. But, as you go about searching for your place, keep in mind that some places are quite exposed and potentially dangerous. Remember also that fear is an ally and strength springs from vulnerability.

The last night, by the firelight, the faces of people in the group have never been more lovely. The masks are gone. Everyone is strong; everyone is weak. You make your vow aloud, along with the others, so that it can be heard. You sacralize and partake of Nature's life blood: water. Now, on the eve of the last night of the severance period, is the time of most severe self-examination. Are you really going to do that to which you have committed yourself? Are you sure about your reasons for doing it? You stand on the brink of the old life.

Before dawn, you are up and moving. Reluctant as you may feel, there is no turning back now. You pack your things. You get your water together. You check in at the "map office" to verify your position with those who will remain at base camp. There is one final ceremony. The ties that bind the group together are severed. The vision questers are formally given over to their separate paths. A few brief hugs, and you are off with your buddy.

You and your buddy eventually separate, at a mutually agreed-upon place. At a point midway between your separate places, the two of you erect a pile of stones, a marker, where you will communicate with each other once a day at different times by leaving some sign to verify your well-being.

At approximately ten o'clock in the morning you say farewell to your buddy. The two of your must now turn your backs on each other and walk to your separate places. For the next three days and nights you will see no one. In the silence of your separateness you will seek your vision.

Aside from the daily responsibility of the stonepile, you are free to be who you want to be. This is the time to forget time, to remember what it is you are seeking and take it into your heart.

When you return on the fourth morning, first to your buddy, waiting at the stonepile, and then to the others at base camp, you will be enacting the role of the mythical hero/ine returning from the threshold. Your reincorporation into the old order, with new status, will begin.

Threshold

Unless a grain fall into the ground and die
It cannot grow into an ear of corn.
Before you died, you had to be awakened.
This is the mystery of Elusis.
—Mysteries of the Seed, *Anonymous*

Before you went to the wilderness you studied the ritualistic devices of various cultures in order to find a means by which to comprehend the experience of the threshold period. Some of these devices are symbols created by the intercourse of the human and the natural; that is, during the next three days and nights you will devise them with the raw stuff provided by the Great Mother. Other of these devices are ritualistic concepts and modes of behavior, drawn from archaic cultures, that also enhance the experience of the threshold. In a sense, these devices are weapons against the forces of darkness. In another way, they are windows, chinks in the cavern, through which the infinite is contacted. In still another way, they are means of focusing and concentrating the attention, of poising and balancing the body in space, of centering the heart in space and time.

The devices of the Vision Quest threshold period are not adapted from any particular belief system. Jungian psychologists would call them archetypes, but they bear the strongest affinity to American Indian culture. The American holy man, Black Elk, in the wisdom of his old age, gave the secret of the *hanblecheyapi,* or "crying for a vision" rite, to a world that someday may comprehend the power and stabilizing influences of Native American rites of transition.

These archetypal devices of the Vision Quest compose a coherent dynamic with which to experience the threshold time, but they are not necessary ingredients. Within each of us lies a gift, a capacity for the spontaneous creation of personally meaningful ritual, which naturally emerges under the conditions of a rite of passage. The Vision Quest provides these conditions.

The Sacred Time

Now you stand alone in the sacred time and all around you are the features of eternity. The mountains mock your flesh and blood. They have been here for a hundred million years. Their incomprehensible age thunders down a symphony of eternity for your ears, a symphony of stillness. For an endless three days and nights you will be unable to escape the silence.

At first, the absence of familiar things within the field of perception creates a huge emptiness, around which the conditioned self flutters like a doomed moth. You set up little projects, little duties to perform, passing the hours in bits and pieces. Your mind races through all the old ruts you left behind.

Eventually you begin to pay attention to eternity. Your heart begins to seek other kinds of nourishment. Small things arrest your eye. You spend more time staring off into space. You hear what the silence is composed of: the varnish of stones, the dark loom of cliffs, the bareness of ridges, the scat of small animals, the mystery of holes in the earth, the flatness of the dust, the sigh of the evening star. The passage of time is marked by the sounds that break the silence: the beating of the heart, the rumble of the stomach, the wind in the trees, the drone of a fly, the distant roar of a jet plane, the flitting of little rat feet in the desert sand.

You will also be aware of other sounds, but you will not know their source. You will hear voices, but you will not see another living soul. The only interpretive instrument you possess is yourself. You may wish to alter your sense of what is real by listening more closely to that which you might other-wise regard as unimportant or unreal.

Now you stand alone. Surely, there can be no end to this ocean of silence you stand at the shore of. You launch yourself, a tiny barque, into the silence, your heart as captain.

The Sacred Place

There was a place deep in the heart of the wilderness that knew you and awaited your arrival. It was necessary that you find this place, or that it find you. Perhaps something drew you—a stone, a plant, an animal, the wind—and you were not able to resist being found.

Here you will hold communion with the Great Mother. You will eat of her sun and drink her air. You will live in her flesh, but you are not a parasite. You will seek to know your place, your function, your reason for being here, upon this earth.

This is the place where you will see how your every action is reflected back on you by the mirror of your environment. Whatever you choose to sow or risk, you will reap with intense self-consciousness. Here is where you will engage in the sacred exchange between human and Nature. Whatever is given to you, you must give back, in your own way. Observe yourself responding to the gifts of Nature; you will learn the nature of the gift that only you can give.

Speak to the powers of your place. Address them respectfully, one and severally. Invoke the spirit of growing things. Ask for strength and patience to endure. Listen to what the wind and the stars and the dead and decaying things tell you. Give a portion of your drinking water to the earth of your place. Remove your shoes and walk barefoot. Caress the hard stones. Go without clothing. Allow your place to become enamored of you. Curl up against the bosom of the Great Mother, until you have warmed the cold earth beneath your body. Dream the dreams of the coyote, the fox, the bear, the lizard, the scorpion, the rabbit, the rattlesnake and the raven. Dream the dreams of the night wind.

The Fast

Food will not pass your lips for three days and nights. You have chosen to fast, to follow a "cloud of witnesses," ancient and modern, who have traveled this ritual path to spiritual insight.

The fasting process is one of readying the soil for a seed to be planted in it. Some call this process self-purification. The seeker empties the body so that the spirit may be filled. By eliminating food from the system, you symbolically encourage death, who waits to fill your emptiness. Living thus in the proximity of death, life is enhanced, made brilliant and terrifying.

A three-day fast does not endanger the body. One can go only a few days without water, but one can go weeks without food. As long as you drink water, the effects of the fast will be mainly psychological. With no meals to organize your day around, you will learn a great deal about your psychological need for structure, and you will discover how much of what you think is physical hunger is really social programming.

The body literally consumes itself on a fast. Such self-consuming burns away the mortal dross, purifying the channels to the soul. Fasting produces such feelings as weakness, intensity, vacancy, fertility, openness, heaviness, lightness, disorientation, harmony and spiritual awarness. Frail and utterly mortal, awkward and exposed, you look into the distance and sense the subtle rolling of the earth. This movement grips you with the nausea of emptiness and yearning. Now you are ready to find truth in the Arapaho vision quest cry: "Great Spirit, have mercy on me. I am starving, I have nothing to eat."

The Stonepile

The heaping of stones is an ancient practice, a symbolic act of communication, a mute affirmation. *This is the way. This is the meeting place. Someone lies buried here. Peace to all who pass.* In parts of the southwestern deserts beside faintly discernible foot trails, archeologists find piles or shrines of heaped stones 10,000 years old.

Each day you will hike over to the stonepile you and your buddy erected. This daily trip is a ritual whereby you formalize your conscious love-link with fellow human beings. Should either of you fail to leave some daily sign at the stonepile, it is the responsibility of one to find out why the other did not respond. If the other is sick, injured, or dying, there is no one other than the buddy who can provide immediate help. No one.

The stones then are symbolic of the fragile, precious link that exists between us all. Though we are separate, unique and alone, our destiny is common, and the earth is shared between us and all living things. We *must* come to love those we are linked with. Without them we would not learn the courage to face death—or to live another day.

The stonepile is a symbol of love. It is constructed at a common border of human responsibility in a beautiful place, where it is easily found.

THE FIRE

In a very real sense, all things are on fire, rusting or otherwise oxidizing slowly or rapidly. Among the by-products of this general oxidation are warmth and light. Necessary for the perpetuation of all life forms, warmth and light are also released from the heart of a human being. Just as the fire of the sun is the heart of our local planetary universe, so the fire of the heart is the center of our local physical universe. As we move through the world with the godlike fire of our hearts, we radiate light and warmth. We are felt by all things.

With this in mind, construct a small fire, a symbol of your heart. Dig a small circular pit. Select your ring stones carefully from the place where you dig. Leave your palm prints on the inside of the pit. Gather just a little dead wood, being careful not to tear away any living branch. In the clean cavity you have made in the earth, you will kindle the fire of your heart. Tend your little fire. Notice how greedily things surrender themselves to the giving of warmth and light. This is the way the heart works.

After the fire has taught you, let it die. The flames have been transferred to your heart. But you must not leave your place without erasing the wound in the earth that you have made. Seal the ashes with soil. Widely scatter the hearthstones. The universe, they say, was born in fire. But no one knows where—or who dug the fire pit. **(Caution)**: Make sure you are not in a restricted area prohibiting the building of campfires.

THE NAME SELF-GIVEN

You did not ask for the name that was given to you. That is because you were not aware to name yourself. Now you have the opportunity to acquire the power and responsibility that comes with a self-naming.

As you walk through the days of the threshold time, seek to give yourself a name that identifies, in the most secret inward shrine of your soul, who you are. Good places to look are within dreams, day dreams and waking visions, at the tops of mountains, down in dark canyons, along the way to the stonepile, under rocks, in the sky, among the plants and animals, in the dirt under your boots. The whole of animate and inanimate existence surrounds you with potential names. The wind that sings in your ears is laden with the syllables of your name.

If you listen and watch closely enough you will discover a secret known by all primitive peoples. Nature is *aware* of you and seeks to speak to you. You may be sitting, pondering a certain problem in your life one morning, when suddenly a hawk will circle your head three times, or an ant will crawl across your hand in a particular way, or a brilliant stone may suddenly appear at your feet. You experience a *connection,* a knowing that has been lost to modern civilized life.

An aspect of your environment that most distresses you—a vicious wind, a thunderstorm, searing heat, bone-chilling cold, a rattlesnake—may in fact become an ally and reveal to you the meaning of your name. Speak to the Great Mother. Tell her that you have come to stay here for a few days and that you desire to learn the lessons which she has for you. But then something must come forth from you—a way of sensing—to embrace what is offered. From this give-and-take is born the mythical creation of your name.

This process of giving oneself a name is potent medicine. The specific object of self-mythology is to transform, or energize, oneself by giving oneself a name or a story. Such transformations and energizings are possible only to the extent to which the namer is willing to assume the name self-given. Those who lend little time, thought or understanding to self-naming invariably derive little benefit from the act. Those who wait before they discover, who strain at the darkness, who grope on their knees among the broken stones, will be rewarded with a mythical destiny that is like a beacon in the night.

THE DREAMING

One of the reasons you came here alone to this place is to dream. Because you came to the Great Mother to experience your dreaming, you must expect, anticipate, and hope that she will speak to you through the countless numbers of dreamers who have been here before you.

Sometimes the dreams of the Vision Quest are singularly clear and powerful. Within them the dreamer finds a name, a story or a mission. Sometimes the dreams are ambiguous and confusing, like a maze, seemingly involving the dreams of many other dreamers. Sometimes the dreams are personal and emotionally demanding. The dreamer awakens in tears, overcome by sudden feeling. Sometimes the dreams surface only vaguely, disturbingly, in the waking mind. Sometimes the dreams come and go like the tides, wreaking their changes on the shore of consciousness, though the dreamer is totally unaware. Many times the dreams occur when the dreamer's eyes are wide open.

Wherever you are, wandering or lying asleep in your bag, attempt to write your dreams down. See them as portents, lessons, messages from the collective unconscious. Notice how your dreams surface into your waking experience weeks, even months, later. The symbols of these dreams can be used to empower your life. The vision quest of life is a search for myths to live by. Dreams are the stuff of which myths can be made.

Dreams point the way. That is, they *are* the way. Our little life, our frail breath, navigates a sea of dreams. There is a very old school of thought which insists that all life is but a dream, that there is no reality apart from this dream. Another equally ancient school of thought insists that all life is but the dream of God. A third school agrees with the first two and adds the notion that you are God.

Are you dreaming or are you awake? Open your eyes and look around you. You are surrounded by natural cycles of waking and sleeping. Even as the spring flower wakes from its slumbering seed, it falls into a dream of endings.

The Circle of Stones

Alone, the aged bushman of the Kalahari Desert waits for death in a circle of thornbushes. When his food is gone and his body too weak to defend, the hyenas break through the circle and the dying is over.

Remember this story as you dwell within the threshold. From the first day, start looking for a place where symbolically you will wait through the last night for death. To this "dying place" you will go ahead of time to prepare "the grave" for occupancy through an all-night deathwatch.

Slowly, carefully, thinking about what you are doing, make a circle of stones in the earth. This circle should be formed exactly as you wish it, but should be large enough to hold your body. Some choose to mark the compass points on the circumference in order to orient themselves to the four cardinal directions.

As the light of the last day of the threshold is swallowed up in darkness, you enter the circle of your grave. Through the night, encompassed by the thornbush of darkness, you wait for death.

If, however, you are given another day by the Great Mother, you will live to see the sun rise. By making yourself ready to die you give birth to yourself. The circle of stones is transformed from a grave to a symbolic vaginal opening in the earth. The dark birth passage is ended. When the dying is done, there is birth. Birth is the coming full circle of death.

Within your circle that last night of the death vigil, you may express yourself as you wish, to pray your prayers and to cry your cries, to throw the desire of your heart into the void of darkness. The womb of the Great Mother embraces you with unknowing. The eyes are blinded by the absence of light. You are pushed and pulled by the unsensed, irresistible forces. Impatience is of no avail. The darkness lingers, punctuated by the cold, infinite gleam of stars, beckoning from the lostness of space. Can it be that Death assumes the mask of an unrequited longing to be filled?

To the south are the warm lands, the calm seas. Would you go there? Would that direction satisfy the rigors of your quest?

To the north are the frozen lands, the cruel seas. Would you go there? Would that satisfy the passion of your quest?

To the west are the dark lands, the silent seas. Would you go there? Would that satisfy the love that seeks to be born in death?

Ahead of you, to the east, the bright lands, the fish-breeding seas. Would you go there? Yes, surely there.

In the time of an eternity, the Great Mother labors to give birth to you. Imperceptibly, you enter the light.

The Cry for a Vision

It is the last night, the night of the deathwatch. You are crouched in your circle of stones, waiting for death, seeking to be born. Look around at the stones of your grave. They are cold. The night wind chills the marrow of your bones. You feel alone, helpless, insignificant, out of place and afraid. Of what use are words, prayers, cries, screams? The silence mocks you with unattain-

47

able eloquence. The stars peer down at you with light generated before human beings ever appeared on the earth.

Do you really believe your cry for a vision will be answered? What right have you to expect it? Are there not many who are more worthy than you? Now is the time to examine your motives for being here, in daring to believe that you shall gain what you desire. The nearest person is far away. There is no one to applaud your piety.

Are you crying for a vision for yourself or for your people? If you cry for yourself alone, the heavens will become impenetrable. Your cry will not extend beyond your own mouth. No one who lives on this earth has any right to cry exclusively for himself. We are all linked. Our destiny is common.

There is no set form as to how or what you should cry. There are a multitude of spiritual disciplines, prayer forms and meditative practices at your disposal. Use any technique with which you feel comfortable. You need not use words. An appropriate cry for a person feeling so deeply that words cannot express is a literal cry, unadorned, unformulated, unhindered by tradition. Just cry out as long and loud and hard as you need to. No one ever said the spiritual quest was either painless or polite.

Cry for love and caring; cry from loneliness. Cry from your helplessness, fear and doubt. Cry for a vision for your people. The world you belong to is filled with people who seek power, but it is not the power of vision. As you lie in the dust like any wretch, dying in your circle of stones, may the cry that goes out from you come from your deepest longing to complete yourself and your world.

Surely, your cry will be answered. The darkness will pass. Dawn will answer your cry. Someday, also, death will dawn. Cry for a vision, then. Cry again and again, until the cry is a grain of sand and you are the mother of pearl.

THE VISION

There is benefit to be gained from seeking a vision, by learning the sacred, solitary postures of countless pilgrims who, from the beginning of human time, have sought to *see*. Questing for a vision, we seek to extend ourselves, to know.

During the three days and nights of the threshold you will seek vision.

But the vision you seek is many different things. Vision is wisdom. Vision is insight into the nature of things. Vision is a deep feeling of balance and harmony with all things. Vision is the ability to see the future. Vision is the ability to dream. Vision is the surging upward of personal creative energy. Vision is transcendent, mystical knowledge – cosmic consciousness. Vision is merely opening the eyes to see what already *is*. Vision is the sight of the sun rising in the east to answer the hope that another day will come. Vision is but a series of small insights into what the meaning of life has been and could be.

However you seek your vision these three days and nights, it is certain that you seek an answer to how you will live the next phase of your life. If you are young, your vision will lead you toward the fullest possible expression of your potential as you enter adult life. If you are an adult, your vision will guide you in the changes necessary for the life transition you face, the crisis you must endure, or the problems you must solve. If you are very much older, your vision will prepare you for the ultimate transition. You may cry for the power to die victoriously and with dignity to enrich, instead of diminish, the lives of those you love.

The Giveaway

After the long last night of your death vigil, when the dawn of a new life shines in your heart, you will return to the others. Somehow your cry has been answered. The light has come. You feel something new in your heart. It is time to look into the eyes of other human beings, your people.

You pack up your things and begin the return by giving away to your place of power. For three days and nights it has given itself away to you. It has taught you the mysteries of natural existence and has provided you with the stuff of survival: fuel for your fire, stones for the fire ring, cover for your head, protection from the cold wind. It has given you a place to lie down in peace. Whatever you have to say to your place, say it now. Give some of your precious water to the place where you built the fire. Sprinkle some on the place where you slept. Erase as many signs of your sojourn as you can.

You cannot expect, however, that your place will remain untouched by your stay. Your presence here has altered it, changed its physical and spiritual composition. Even hundreds or thousands of years from now, though the physical signs be obliterated, something of you will remain here. You may elect to give away the cardinal stones of your circle to your place; that is a fitting gesture. Those who went before us left circles in the earth.

Soon you will be enveloped in human warmth and laughter. Arms will open. Words will fill the air. Love will be reflected in the eyes of those around you who have come back from their own quests. Try to plan and enact a ritual of giving to each, one by one, something from your heart. It can be a stone, a dried flower, a hug, a poem, a few words, a song. It is dangerous to receive holy power without channeling its flow to others. You may not feel particularly powerful or holy, but only filled with gratitude to be back with the others. It is the *willingness* to be a channel, to perform a symbolic giveaway that matters. For some, the power of the vision transforms them into a channel for its communication. For others, the humble effort to become a channel is what creates the vision.

Now it is time to look back. Your buddy is waiting at the stonepile. Just a little ways further, across the ridge and up the wash, you will see the others, waiting for your return. Give yourself to loneliness now, so that you can give yourself to them.

Reincorporation

We returned to our places, these kingdoms
No longer at ease here, in the old
dispensation,
With an alien people clutching their gods.
—T. S. Eliot, "Journey of the Magi"

The return from Death Valley takes twelve hours. If the weather is bad on the Sierra passes, we take the Isabella cutoff, which means Bakersfield and 350 miles of Interstate 5. As the miles unwind the talk shifts in focus from what has taken place to what lies ahead at home. The freeway is grimy and choked with cars and semis. The terrain flattens out, becomes gray with smog. North the four-lane freeway runs toward home, level and straight all the way to the redolent cattle corrals and slaughterpens of Stockton.

It is necessary to return, to go back across the threshold and encounter the world that, for a brief eternity, you left behind. But it is never quite possible to go back to the same place: "Into the same river we step and do not step" (Heraclitus). For a while, this world will seem unappetizing, different, even terrifying. It moves on in its metal ruts and seems to care little for those who have been on a Vision Quest. Everyone is immersed in the grim day-to-day business of survival. No one seems to speak your language. It is not the civilized world that has changed, however, but yourself. A week ago you severed from this world; you left it as though it were dead. Now you come back to it, a stranger with a vision.

This reincorporation can precipitate a crisis. You tense against the impact of social boundedness, the laws of human space, time and conduct, the claustrophobia of four walls and a roof, even the too-soft embrace of a bed and mattress. The tension produces the same kind of gut-wrenching fear you felt the night before you stepped across the threshold. Again, you must confront the basic questions of birth, survival and death.

For a while, you may experience both elation and alienation. You can still feel the sun in your eyes and the wind in your hair. But when you try to tell others about it, they do not understand, or do not seem to care. They seem threatened by your new-found joy. While you were gone, they were absorbed in their own battles with dragons. They were living their own lives. Inevitably, they cannot know what you have been through, unless they actually try it themselves. You realize that the only way to communicate the experience is not to talk about the vision, but to live it.

With the dew still fresh in your hair, it is easy to live the vision. Who has seen the unbounded horizon and not been, at least for a time, unbounded? At first, you are buoyed up by the vividness of your recent adventure. You experience a great love and fondness for your place of power. You feel at home in your body. Your senses are alert and active. From the realm of the gods you have come to this mortal world like the mythical protagonist. Where are the dragons to slay? Where are the trials, now that you have strength to face them?

The true power of the Vision Quest cannot be measured except in terms of the process of reincorporation. Only when the vision is tried by existence in the mortal world is its true worth known. Yet the time must inevitably come when you wake up in the morning and realize that you will not be able to maintain the vision. Though you did your best to keep the flame alive, it flickers now.

This is a critical time. You can either let the flame die, or you can decide to begin the vision quest of your life and seek the places where there is fuel to feed your fire. Truly, the quest has just begun. The hero/ine has just returned from the realm of the gods with the spark of life that will kindle the spirit of a dying world. The world, however, does not care.

The hero/ine sees the magnitude of the task that lies ahead. The dragons, overawed at first by the shining presence of the protagonist, had shrunk back into the shade. Now seeing, after all, that the protagonist is a mere mortal, they sally forth, their mouths belching fire. Their names are the same as the dragons of the Vision Quest. They are fear, anxiety, boredom, emptiness, impatience, self-doubt and lack of faith. Encompassed by the likes of these and separated from the healing influences of the Great Mother, the hero/ine feels reluctant to set foot on the trail of the vision quest of life.

The journal entry of one reincorporated Vision Quester speaks for the experience of many.

Why can't I remember the revelation? Why can't I feel the free-dom? Why is it lost? In no way did I intend this loss of vision, this doubt, this descent from the mountain top. I *fell!* There must be a kind of spiritual gravity. Such energy it takes to struggle up toward the Vision! Such self-examination. Such effort it takes to break through into the illuminating insights, and with what ease we fall after the Quest is over. Why? Why?

The hero/ine must face the fall because there is no other law of the mortal world more powerful than the law of change. As "time and chance happeneth to us all," so the returning vision quester must face the fact of change. What is light must become dark, even as day becomes night. What is full must become empty, even as summer becomes winter.

Every spiritual tradition teaches the inevitability, even the *necessity,* of the darkness that follows or accompanies illumination. As the devout believer "comes closer to God," he is sorely beset by the Devil. As the initiate into the mystery enters "the unveiled presence of the most high," she is warned that possession of the secret is dangerous; it will bring great difficulty, even death. For every spiritual action there is a mortal reaction. The opposite of the spiritual is the mundane. The opposite of illumination is ignorance. As the yogi says, "After *samadhi,* we sweep the floor." The Zen master prepares his pupils by teaching: "Before *satori* the mountain is just a mountain and the river is just a river. During *satori,* the mountain is no longer a mountain and the river is no longer a river. After *satori,* the mountain is just a mountain and the river is just a river."

The hero/ine learns to live in two worlds. This is perhaps the most important teaching of the Vision Quest. One world is sacred, spiritual, eternal. It is the world you stepped into when you crossed the threshold. The other world is mortal, material and subject to change. It is the world you stepped into when you recrossed the threshold. The first world is where your vision is conceived; the second world is where you give birth to your vision. As William Blake put it, "Joys impregnate. Sorrows bring forth."

When the Vision Quest ends, the vision quest of life begins. The terms of this quest are that one learns to walk in balance between two worlds, that one seeks to conceive and then to give birth to vision. The willingness to be a channel of vision takes great courage and endurance and is not lightly assumed. There will be times when you stumble and fall. Then you will want to crawl away to the sacred mountains. These are the times of the greatest potential, when you are looking the dragons square in the eye.

Only you know what you have hidden away, growing steadily and surely with its magical roots in your subsoil. As you grow, the vision grows. There is no other way.

BOOK 3

3. THE PEOPLE

I implore you . . . to submit to your own myths.
Any postponement in doing so is a lie.
—William Carlos Williams, Paterson

Most of those who have participated in the Vision Quest and who have helped write this book are residents of Marin County, California, the suburban "paradise" at the northern end of the Golden Gate. Behind the closed doors of this respectable community lurk loneliness and desperation. Behind the symbolic affluence and easy living there rages a hunger that cannot be filled. Teenagers cruise the streets, symbolically acting out their parents' restless search for fulfillment and meaning.

The children grow up in a protected, superficially pleasant environment. They become adolescent and are caught between childhood and adulthood in a long holding pattern until, as if by magic, they become adult at the age of twenty-one. As adults they enter the ranks of the working people. They find a job, a niche somewhere; they fall in and out of love and divert themselves in a variety of ways from the daily bumper-to-bumper commuting, the rising costs of living, the horrors of the newspapers. They marry or cohabitate; they do or do not bear children; they do or do not buy a hot tub or participate in the human potential movement. They separate or divorce or grow older, into the rocky transitions of middle age, and wake up one morning to the fact that there are wrinkles on their bodies that cannot be erased by a rolfing, a sauna, a new haircut, a *sans soleil* tan or a pill. They wonder what their life has amounted to. They think about going somewhere else. They become grand-parents, join the "seniors," retire, find themselves in a rest home. Many of them retain much of their youthful vigor and are wise, but they are largely ignored by the rest of the community. Many of them become very lonely. They do or do not prepare themselves for death. They die.

The people of Marin County live their life as people everywhere do. Some of them live by myths that are fleeting and transient, created by the mass media or current fashion. Others live by myths that are profoundly spiritual. When combined, all these myths by which people live describe the essence of a culture.

Because of our Vision Quest work we have become acquainted with the mythical essence of Marin County. Those who are intrigued by the Vision Quest, attend the preparatory meetings, and then go on the quest, are expressing in their unique ways this mythical essence.

From the beginning, when I first spoke with people about enacting a Vision Quest ritual, there were those who seemed automatically to understand.

> When I first heard the idea I knew it was for me. I can't say why I knew so well. But even when I was a little boy the times of being alone, all by myself, were especially powerful. I got a hidden, deep, sensual thrill from knowing I was alone, and free to be whoever I wanted to be.
> — Creosote, age 34

It is probably true that such a response to the challenge of a rite of passage such as the Vision Quest is due to an ancestral knowing, deeply etched in the collective archetypal memory. Yet there were many who were attracted who could not have put it into such fancy words.

> I thought, a Vision Quest? All alone, without food, crying my lungs out? Am I crazy? Do I want to do that? My friends said I was insane. . . . It was the *challenge* that made me do it.
> — I'd Pick a Daisy, 15

There was no particular class of person or personality that took up the challenge. The juvenile offender, bored and defiant behind the bars of juvenile hall, was as compelled as the lonely woman whose children were grown and husband divorced. The housewife and the burned-out professional responded as eagerly as the artist seeking vision or the old man dreaming dreams. They may have had different reasons for questing for a vision, but they all shared one common attribute: they were willing to put their bodies on the line, to step across the threshold.

The memory of their faces returns to me: sunburned faces smeared with dirt, honest and uncontrived faces stained with healing tears. Nature undid their guises, turning their eyes into silence, their ears into wind, their bodies into animals, and their souls into waterholes. The wilderness had entered them while they were alone and starving with nothing to eat. The force of that entry, irresistibly gentle as the pressure of sunlight, faulted, folded and uplifted them like the mountains they stood on. The Great Spirit of the Universe had heard their cry and had sent the bellies of their souls something to eat: dawn.

COMPANION OF THE WIND

Companion of the Wind was fourteen when he went with us into the White Mountains to Vision Quest. Though he was young in age, he had been readied by his life. His mother and father were divorced; the mother was crippled by polio. He was holding down a job as a busboy at a restaurant and holding up his family. He saw it as a ritual that would symbolize his attainment of maturity. He went because he felt that he was ready to become a man.

He chose an exposed 12,000 foot ridge overlooking Cottonwood Basin, his only companions the thin, cold wind and an ancient, twisted, mostly-dead stump of bristlecone pine. He did not want to hole up like a turtle and wait through the trial. With touching, idealistic courage he said goodbye. He was ready to face the worst of it.

The warm mornings turned cold every afternoon. Clouds gathered and scudded dark and low across the treeless ridges. Rain threatened. Thunder whispered in the southeast. His journal says he spent one night crying. His journal also contains a remarkable dialogue with the wind, a sacred exchange between himself and Nature that was carried on intermittently for two days and nights.

Wind, can you help me on my Vision Quest?

Yes.

I have so many questions to ask. Who am I? Why am I here on this planet? What is my name? How can I help my family?

You will receive two names, one I will give you and the other you shall give to yourself. The one I shall give you is Companion of the Wind. You may share this with your friends and relatives. The one you give to yourself shall be for your sake alone. As long as you remember this you shall be able to know the answers to all your questions. As for the other questions you have asked me, I will help you find the answers on the last night.

I thank you, Wind. I also think I love you.

There is one last thing you should remember. I am always listening but not always speaking.

I will remember. Wind, there is one last thing I ask of you.

Yes?

Will you protect me from anything that might ruin my Vision Quest?

I will protect you until your day has come.

I thank you, Wind.

He learned to put up his tarp so tight it would not clatter in the wind. But he was cold, so cold he could never get quite warm. He missed his family and felt sad. Once, when the wind died down, he stuck several dollar bills between the needles of the branches of the bristlecone and took a picture of them, bedecked with a sign: MONEY TREE. But mostly he talked to the wind and thought about what it meant to be an adult: "I feel much better about myself. I think I am beginning to understand more about myself and everything else. Maybe this is what the Indians thought was adulthood. I must also remember what my friend Allan told me: 'An adult is just a child with responsibilities.'"

The evening of his last night the sky flared up with a most unusual high altitude sunset, transforming the white limestone of the mountains with fiery orange and red. He built his circle and sat down inside it to keep his vigil and to speak with the wind, which by now was a beloved and trusted friend.

I think it is time to build my circle. How big should I make it? Since I'm not going to sleep in it I'll make it big enough to sit in. What rocks should I use? . . . I'll just pick out the rocks that work best.

There, it looks pretty good. Maybe the Wind will speak to me and answer some of my questions.

Wind, I am here in my circle and wish to speak to you. I want to ask you some questions that I've been thinking about. Why am I here, Wind? What purpose do I have in this world?

How can I control my emotions, like anger, fear, and all the others, so that they will help me instead of tearing me apart. How can I make my family happier? Teach me to understand them. Please!

Your purpose is to help and make happier the people on earth.

Who am I, Wind?

Take off your ring. What shape is it?

It is a circle.

What are you sitting in?

A circle.

How many sides does a circle have?

It doesn't have any sides.

Good. Now, where does it end?

It doesn't have an ending.

You are right.

But what does this have to do with the questions I'm asking you?

Have patience and listen. I am like a circle. I have no ending. You are also like a circle. In your cycle you have no ending. But when my cycle ends, your cycle ends.

Why is this?

Because you are a part of me and I am a part of you. Remember this: when our circles end, the world ends. Understand the circle and you will understand yourself. As for your emotions, you do not want to control them, but to understand them. Then you will be able to deal with them. This goes the same with people.

Wind, how do you know these questions before I ask them?
Remember, I am a part of you and you are a part of me. Now go and enjoy your surroundings. Tonight I will speak to you again.
Thank you, Wind.
You are welcome, Companion of the Wind.

The wind blew him back to base camp the following day; he bore two new names, one public, one private. He declared he felt secure in himself, and looked it. He had proved something to himself that no one could take away. Some months later we asked him if he could remember the private name the wind had given him. "Oh yes," he replied, as if we had asked him a very silly question.

For this young man the Vision Quest was a rite of passage in the traditional sense. Symbolically he left childhood behind and went out alone, facing his fears and his destiny, to find in the spirit of Nature an ally and a name. In the same manner, hundreds of young Marin County men and women have come to Rites of Passage, challenged by the opportunity to enact a rite of passage to formalize their passing from childhood to adulthood.

Each youth carefully prepared for, then entered, the silence. Each was a world unto her/himself. They would show up for meetings at schools and churches, intense, naive, full of energy. When they talked about the Vision Quest, I could see them weighing the idea in their minds. (Can I do that? Has my upbringing prepared me to undertake such a challenge?) Many went even though they were not certain they could do it. Many succeeded in staying out three days and nights without food. Some returned early, for a variety of reasons. They kept journals, in most cases fragmentary and episodic, but filled with life and emotion. Their voices return on the wind, in scraps and pieces.

My buddy and I sat beside our rockpile, our only means of communication, and wept before we departed. I think we're both feeling many anxieties and fears, that ahead of us lies a huge question mark.
—Free Bird, 17

I'm starving. I'm very weak and I just feel like sleeping. But I can't

sleep. My back aches from lying on this hard surface for two days.
. . . I find myself daydreaming about food: oranges, hard-boiled
eggs, fresh bread, anything. . . .

Oh please let the sun set. Please, please, *please!* I feel so god-
damned empty. I can't wait until I encounter society again. Isn't
that what this is all about?
—I'd Pick a Daisy, 15

The thunder is shaking and I am scared. . . . I sure hope that there
are no flash floods. Don't rain, please. I am not ready for rain. I want
someone to hold me. I feel lonely, very lonely now that those rain
clouds are coming. . . . I hate the fact that all I can do is sit and wait,
sit and wait. I can *feel* what loneliness is. . . . I HOPE IT DOESN'T
RAIN! I'm not the homesick type, but I would give almost anything to be with my parents.
—Weak Stomach, Strong Heart, 17

It's all so lonely and cold, so long and drawn out, eternity, black,
endless tunnels and no time for food or love and I miss my lover
very much. My heart is aching and it's all getting so dark I can't see
her in front of me anymore. . . . So many empty thoughts floating
by—my past, my future, etc. I know I'll live. I know I'll survive.
Wind howling now, howling, howling. So cold are my hands. . . .
—Moon Song Crying, 17

Today I made my circle and named myself Lone Stone Among the
Rest. . . . Then later this afternoon I sang my name and walked
around my circle. Doing this gave my name more depth and meaning. After I had been walking around my circle I had to quit because
I was losing my balance. I started singing it again, when I got to my
place overlooking the valley. I started to cry, yet I continued. My
name symbolizes my cutting the line connecting me to my parents,
making me a separate and unique human being.
—Lone Stone Among the Rest, 17

La montana de la vision is high; it took me four hours to conquer. It
won't allow just anyone to reach its crown. Sweat, thirst and in-

tense heat try my stamina. Still I climb. My pack is heavy; it bur-
dens my back with pain. Perspiration rolls down my body. I'm going
through hell, but soon I will reach the heaven awaiting me. I stand
on the top. A cool breeze welcomes me. I feel accepted. I look far
below. *La Bahia de la Concepcion* rests in the earth like a babe in
mother's arms. The Sea of Cortez shines in the East. I feel very
close to the heart of the mountain. Its power is inside me. It is
strong and spiritual. Never will it cease to be.
—Linda, 16

These are the voices of children becoming strong. They are beginning to see
into the life of things. They are beginning to assume the burden of heroism in
this world. They are engaged in the sacred task of creating a survival myth for
themselves and their world. They must find their own way.

I must even let my own son go to a place somewhere out on the eastern
flank of White Mountain Peak. Right now he is battening his tarp down
against a hailstorm. For cover he is using a thick stand of mountain mahogany
and the good sense to get low if there is lightning. All I can do is trust that he
is all right.

Crisp and cold. I awoke with a bloody nose. I'm tired today; my
energy is gone. I sit in darkness surrounded by light. My eyes see
beauty, but my bones feel death is near. My mind tells me that soon
I shall rejoin and rejoice with my people.

I get cold so easily. The silence of the place makes me hear
the ringing of my ears. I imagine I see wisps of smoke in the trees —
hallucinating, maybe. I think maybe I'm seeing the spirits of long-
dead Indians still using this land.

Oh, the wind is cold when it blows across my body; it makes
me feel so alien — though why should this be? My ancestors lived
with the land for hundreds of thousands of years. But I feel so puny,
so exposed, like the spark of life within me is so small.
—Keenan, 16

Fire Stick

Rich, a burly, clean-cut, handsome young man with a slight Armenian accent, showed up at a Rites of Passage meeting at the local high school. When he also attended the next meeting, we could see that he was hooked. Yet he hardly seemed part of the group, even when at the last meeting before we left for the wilderness, he held hands in a circle with the rest of us. Rich was not easy to get to know. There was something aloof about him, something that seemed to annoy others in the group.

A month after Companion of the Wind had vision quested, we were back in the same White Mountains. It was mid-August. On the floor of the Owens Valley the temperature was in the nineties. At 12,000 feet there was a chill in the air, and menacing clouds appeared in the west. That night around the campfire Rich began to talk more about himself.

He was a "jock." Not only was he the best high hurdler in the league, but he was also all-conference fullback and homecoming king. And he was a loner. He spoke of being unable to enjoy the fads and frivolities of his peers. He spoke of high personal ideals, of becoming a lawyer or a doctor someday. He spoke of drive and hustle and challenge. It was easy to see that he placed less value on love and sentimentality than on ambition and competition. He said, "I don't need anybody. I have learned to get along by myself." Looking Through the Eyes of a Hawk (17), who had been on a previous Vision Quest, replied: "Tell us that when you come back from being alone." "O.K.", he said, taking up the challenge.

And then, as if to cement his resolve, he requested my permission to leave for his quest one night early. Already he had begun to fast to intensify his experience, and his request seemed to indicate that, like the high hurdler, he wanted to be out in front. I told him he should first check it out with the group. His buddy agreed to accompany him to his power place and set up a stonepile the two of them could check the following morning. The group gave its consent with varying degrees of enthusiasm. I felt it was a bit unfair to the others, but nobody seemed to object.

So Rich went out one night early. That same night, after everyone had gone to bed early to be up and off at the crack of dawn, the heavens fell down. In the midst of clouds so thick you could see no further than a hundred feet, a lightning storm occurred. It was a godawful storm that would not let go. The flashes of lightning bolts glowed eerily in the thick gloom. Thunder cracked and howled and leaped from the fog, and there seemed no end of it. Finally hail and sleet fell until our tarps were laden to the bursting point, and fell some more. Out there in the gloom we could hear a couple from the group singing the Beatles', "Here Comes the Sun." We were all cold and wet and miserable, but something deep inside us was excited. We called out to each other in the dark: "Are you guys all right?"

Just before morning the storm subsided. We awoke to a clear cold dawn. Whiteness lay all around. Somebody said, "I wonder how Rich is doing?" Rich was writing in his journal.

Last night I experienced what our leaders had warned us all to be prepared for—severe thundershowers, hail and the whole bit. I was blessed by the fact that I had discovered a natural shelter. I'm quite proud of myself and how I reacted to the situation. I didn't panic. . . . I can't believe I survived the night. I started thinking about the group, how they were probably scared, especially Steven. I know he hates lightning. I wonder if they're thinking about me? Anyway I'm real happy. . . . I thought about everybody last night. I felt emotional. No—that isn't true. I am emotional, but I'm afraid to express myself. . . . I seem to be adjusting O.K. I feel very close to all of the other vision questers. But somehow I'm not allowing myself to become too compatible. Friendships and relationships are hard for me. . . . I'd love to return from the Vision Quest filled with such joy and love and compassion and just let down my guard and love people and accept them.

DAY TWO
One thing I've learned: the day sure is long. I dozed off yesterday evening, and when I awoke I couldn't figure out whether it was morning or evening. The sun was still shining. Last night I was overcome with loneliness, fatigue and hunger. I wept. It hailed again last night. I thank god for providing such superb shelter. I miss the family. I can't seem to get my mind off them. I can't wait to get back and see Gail, Dad, Jr. and everybody. The mountains seem to be staring at me. They must realize that I'm an oddity. I can't help feeling I've invaded their territory, that I have no right

being here. They said they understand what I'm going through. They accept me.

God, am I ever tired. Sometimes I dread having to go to the stonepile. The trek involves climbing precipitous rocks, ledges and crevices. My hands are all scraped. I fear that at the height of my fatigue I may fall to my death. Last night while lying in my shelter I observed the rock formation that encompassed me. I noticed that one gigantic rock was set on three points of smaller rocks. I imagined how death would feel if the gigantic rock were to fall on me in the night. I imagined that it would be a real warm experience, very painless, and that the rock would choke my last living breath out of me and I would fly away. I would take the form of an eagle and fly away.

I can't overcome this intense feeling of loneliness. I keep thinking I won't make it. But I know I just have to. The day is so long. The sun never seems to set. I'm very hungry. I just can't go to sleep. I cried tonight. I cried because I'm real lonely. I've never experienced anything so awful. I'm not scared and I can overcome hunger, but the loneliness is too intense. It haunts me. I can't wait to get home. I just can't wait. I'm trying to think of ways to cope with my loneliness, but there aren't any. The time goes by so slow. I never leave my area unless I go to the rock pile. I just sit and wait for the day to end, but it never does. I wonder if anyone else is feeling this lonely. I will never do anything like this again in my whole life. Please God, help me make it through the night. . . .

Day Three

Last night, before I built my fire, I was in a desperate state. I couldn't stop thinking lonely thoughts. More than once I thought of turning back. . . . During the night I had a lot of dreams. These dreams were very much the same as the dreams I've had every night since I've been here. They involve teachers and students I knew at my other school before I moved. . . . I've decided to keep busy today to keep my mind clear. Today I will construct my circle. I will die in the presence of Mother Nature! She will witness the rebirth of a new soul.

I have realized during my Vision Quest that I am a very

lucky person. I live with people that love me and I love the people I'm living with. Only this experience could have brought this realization out of me. The test will be when I return.

Fire flashes through my mind. How comfortable I feel when I sit next to my fire. I feel strong again. It is very rejuvenating. I've decided to name myself Fire Stick. Perhaps it is an indication of my fate. Will I die in fire? Will I burn in hell? Or has a burdened, weather-beaten flame been rekindled to warm and comfort my life forever?

The next morning when he returned there was no question that he was part of the group. He was a like a big, happy puppy, wagging his tail and hugging everybody. Love, pure and strong, came through him and suffused us with happiness.

I have returned. All feelings of loneliness and hunger have perished. The joy of returning to base camp was overwhelming. Such a feeling of happiness and warmth. Somehow my feelings of loneliness are gone. It's over and I'm glad. Tomorrow I continue my life. I will never forget my Vision Quest. I still miss my family. It's too bad that they will never really understand what I have been through. It can't be expressed through words. It's a feeling experience. I feel sad for some reason, perhaps because at my camp I was really in tune with myself. I felt empty and pure. Will the Vision Quest alter my life?

At the Vision Quest reunion three weeks later he brought his journal to share with us. He had added a postscript.

The ultra-high I experienced on my Vision Quest is one I have not been able to duplicate since. Although I feel as though I have failed the expectations I promised to fulfill on the last night of my Vision Quest (the height of my emotionalism), these I have learned:

I have shared two conditions that unfortunately exist widely in this world—hunger and loneliness. I have shed the mask that shielded me from being my true person. I have realized that in the past I elevated myself to false heights of virtuousness and morality, and that I am no better than my peers, beneath them in many respects. I have also shared the most profound experience of all my life with a group of people that I respect and love tremendously. These feelings will remain with me always.

Among the young, the Vision Quest is a ritual to formalize the transition from childhood to adulthood. Among adults, the Vision Quest formalizes other life transitions. The older people who come with us recognize how growth requires little deaths and rebirths. They are willing to confront what they fear. They step onto the path with courage, having arrived at a place in their lives where three days and nights in the desert without eating, symbolically seeking a vision of self-transformation, appeals to them.

GIFT BEARER

Virginia, a former professor of social and cultural anthropology, came to us two years after her beautiful husband, to whom she had committed herself as though to God, had died of cancer. He had died a happy, brave death, with his loved ones gathered around him. In the intervening years she had also sought to die, to join him, not by committing suicide, but by rationally seeking with her whole being to die, as did the aborigine or the Eskimo. She relinquished her possessions to her children and loved ones, set a date for her death, and concentrated all her energy and the energy of those who loved and understood her on the moment of her death.

The moment came, and passed. As she had secretly feared, she did not die, but fell instead into a deep sleep. During her sleep she dreamed that a dark figure in a black hooded cloak appeared before her and forcibly pushed her back into life. For a long time she would not accept the verdict of her dream and fell into a deep depression.

She came to the Vision Quest with a complex and unhappy heart, yet conducted herself with the understanding and deliberation of a first-rate anthropologist in the field. The power and direction of her quest drew her to the most barren place, destitute of any growing thing, in the blood-colored hills of the volcanic, waterless Saline Range in southeastern California.

For two days a violent sandstorm smothered the face of the desert. In this place of power, deliberately chosen because it closely resembled what she was feeling inside, she sought ritually to reach across the void of death to contact her dead husband. A foreigner to the deserts of the southwest and a long-time resident of Florida, she disappeared into the wind with her buddy, wearing a T-shirt saying, "It's Better in the Bahamas."

I came to my place and put down my pack. Without thinking, I took one of the sticks I had brought—my "snake stick"—from the mesquite spring on the way here. It was in my left hand. I knew I had to make an Invocation to my place. I stood in the center of the ancient stone circle, faced east, then west, then north, then south. This is what I called out, as nearly as I can remember:

Hear me, Place. I have come to spend three days and three nights in You and be with You.

As I face the east, I ask that you grant me light—let the Light of Love be shed upon me.

As I face the west, I ask you to teach me to die gracefully so that the richly colored sunset beams may bless the hearts of those I love.

As I face the north, I ask that you give me your strength—the strength of your barren mountains, your rocky ridges. Send me a lodestone vision that will last me the rest of my life.

As I face the south, I ask that you grant me your blessings of gentleness. Stark and sere as you look, I know you can confer the sweetness and softness I have known so well in the warm seas, in the gentle surges over coral reefs. Grant me the gift of your gentleness.

When I was finished I wept, standing in the circle. Then I put the water jugs in the shade. I spoke to the spaces in the rock pile where I intended to build my shelter. I said:

"Snake, I have come to spend three days and three nights in this spot. If you are in there, please do not harm me and I will not harm you. If you are here, speak now."

Then I poked in all the holes with my stick. There was no rattle. (A tiny insect just landed on my hand as I wrote. I realize I must not kill any living thing while I am here. Not an insect, nor any

creature. Ask them to leave me, yes. Swat them, no.)
Now I will build my shelter.

But the wind-whipped sand seethed through her shelter and forced her to find another place, a fissure, deep enough for her body and out of the full force of the wind.

> I took the cup of water and made my invocation telling why I was here, what I wanted to learn and experience, and asking the permission of the fissure spirits and the snake people, if such there be in that place, to stretch my tarp for shade over the depression. Then I drank three swallows of my water, spilled three swallows onto the ground at the center of the depression, and drank the rest. I asked for a sign if I was not welcome there. Now I will begin the work. If I am not welcome, the sign will come as I try to erect the tarp.
> The wind is powerful again tonight. On the lee side of the huge rock pile, it is only eddies. When they drop off for a moment I can hear the sound of the wind in the wide, barren valley. It is a hissing sound, very like the sound of a distant rushing river. I could swear there are cataracts rushing through the empty canyons between my perch and the far ridge to the west.
> As I hear the wind blowing across the darkening mountains I am reminded of yesterday's lesson – and gift – the desiccation and defleshing of attachments to the past that would prevent my clean dying. Again the burning sensation under the breastbone. Though I am not so mercilessly exposed to the defleshing wind, it reminds me of its surgery of yesterday. This is different from "letting go." One's umbilical cords must be defleshed and withered. There are some you cannot just let go of. Yesterday the cords were burnt, dried up, preparing for freedom from the past. Today it was: "Sit. Wait." Tomorrow? I have prepared my prayer. I have spoken it to the circles.

As the bleak desert wind dried up her attachments to the sorrow and bereavement of her recent past, her love for her husband held and grew in the soilless rock that edges the chasm of Death. But how could she reach her husband? It seemed some transformation was necessary, some kind of rebirth that would bring her wholly to death.

The silence is deafening! This is a day of utter motionlessness. Yesterday the terrible desiccating wind and grit. Today the absolute stillness, the incredible motionlessness. What is her (Mother Nature's) message today? Don't move? Be still? Do not act? My head aches. Two very fat black flies with striped shoulders buzz my shelter. They buzz but do not bite, and when they land on my bedpad they are utterly motionless for minutes. It seems I have waited so long. How can the Great Spirit require yet more stillness, more utter motionlessness?

I check my watch—and realize how ridiculous that is. I am bored, wanting this trial and these discomforts to be over—and embarrassed because I am bored. I feel inadequate, dull; I despair of a vision. I despair of the change I so desire. I am not to be transformed—any more than these mountains. I will go on forever, the gray half-life stretching to eternity. Even those words of despair I have written a hundred times over in the last three years. There is nothing new, neither a new pain nor a new joy. Even the brief joys . . . I know to be ephemeral even as I feel them. My head aches with my boring sameness. I am bored with being me. *Then be someone else.* But how? *The variations of life are infinite.* I know, but how does that help me be someone else? *Come back into me and let me put you out again in a new form.* How can I do that except die physically? *Sit. Wait.* Hoping for the change? *Stop hoping. Just sit. Wait.*

For three days and nights she sat and waited through the wind storm, settling into the earth like a stone. As her umbilicals to the past were "defleshed," she began to see that part of herself which remained fresh and intact, and that part which was dying.

I do not feel alone. I am surrounded by spirits. They are neither friendly nor unfriendly. They exert their power over me at the behest of the Great Spirit. They are incisive. They clean my soul. They cut the restraining cord, drawing all the pulsing blood-

72

energy from it, drying it, withering it, releasing the energy that has been stored there.

The life energy from the wellspring of my past is being drawn out, released. My past life – love – is becoming desiccated, preserved, like a corpse found in hot desert sands, still with incredibly legible detail – or like a dried flower, still with color and shape and beauty but without the need for food or water, with no drawing upon the energies of love which know no past or present or future and spend themselves as easily upon memories as upon present relationships.

Perhaps with this ancient psychic surgery I will be able to love Aldie [husband who has recently died] now as he is coming to love me, free of the yearning for the shape and color of our past love. I can love Aldie in and through the loves of the present, whatever they are or will become. Nothing of the old love, the dead love, the dying self is lost; the body is preserved in all its beauty forever unchanging, its spirit free to create further bodies – to the glory of the Spirit of the WE, the glue of the new, the microcosm of the macrocosmic social structure birthing itself.

With the realization that she could love her dead husband through the loves of her present life, she awoke to the morning of the third day.

One of my prayers has been answered! So now my cry, my prayer is: "Teach me how to become the Gift, that I may take it to my People in death."

It is exciting to realize that we come into this physical and social dimension in order to fashion a gift, an enrichment, an addition. It has always seemed so one-way before. This awareness strengthens my belief that my gift will have to do with the *way* of dying.

I feel at peace, content. My questions have been answered. I can accept my alone-life, knowing its purpose. Interaction, *love*, is the purpose and the core. Now I see the possibility of a different kind of interaction – and it is something I can start to learn as soon as I get home, beginning with my little place/house and my plants. How to interact with people this way I do not yet know.

73

She returned from her quest with a name, Gift Bearer. She joined us in our work and asked not to be paid. She bore love to us, and a strange kind of joy.

SOLO

Natalie, a psychotherapist, became interested in the Vision Quest when she conducted in-staff training at the old Rites of Passage, when it was still a drug abuse outfit. She had all eight of us get down on our knees in front of a big piece of butcher paper, gave us crayons, and said, "Draw your life myth." We did. I looked at the incredible mural we had created and understood none of it, except for my own picture. Then she said, "Connect your life myth with all the other life myths." That was a bit more difficult. Eventually, we did that too. And by connecting our myths to each other we formalized and came to understand a common purpose.

Several years before, Natalie had chosen to uproot herself, leave her marriage and Boston home of twenty years, and hit the road for California. She started a new life there, designing her own work, making new friends, and shedding a great deal of her material past. For a woman brought up within the "woman's place is in the home" tradition, her solitary move to California represented a great leap into the unknown. What she desired above all was the right to be herself.

As an artist, a dancer, a student of consciousness and an emotional adventurer, she brought all of herself to her work. When she heard about the Vision Quest, she was hooked. She gracefully bore herself through a series of meetings with an oversized, rambunctious bunch of kids at an alternative high school; she took notes, absorbed in her own careful preparation.

It was Eastertime in the Funeral Mountains, and the wind was full of cold fury. A storm had come down from Alaska. The snows caught on the teeth of the Sierra Nevada, but the wind came on unchecked, across the Inyos and the Saline Valley, up over the Panamints and down into the great wind-catcher of Death Valley. The temperature went down to freezing at night, making ice in our plastic water jugs.

The night before the threshold time, as the group sat and talked, I went into an uncontrollable fit of shivering and shuddering. I could not unclench myself from a vague, overpowering dread. Natalie heaped her sleeping bag upon me and lay down upon my shuddering body with her weight and warmth, until I lay calm. The next morning she went into the wind.

To grasp it, the reality-unreality of it, I need to write. I am fortunate that I am out of the cold wind, in a spot not far from our base camp. There are no trees nor large bushes on the whole horizon. What faces me is a bare mountain, stone, sagebrush, and craggy rocks jutting upward. My god! What *am* I doing here, alone for three days to come, with only water? . . . I've never slept outside alone anywhere and here I am in the middle of the most barren of places for three days alone without food. It is a challenge! . . .

This is sobering, very sobering. As I walked away from my warm, cave-like shelter, I was stepping lightly, feeling carefree. Suddenly I froze stiff as I saw before me a coiled snake, black tail upward, body rigid, waiting to strike. It was about sixteen inches long, sandy colored, exactly the hue of the pink-brown earth. It had dark stripes and a small, triangular head. . . . It looked more like what I remember as a copperhead than a rattlesnake. Its black tail did not appear to have rattles on it, but I was paralyzed with fright and not sure what I saw. I stared: it was powerful, poised, ready to strike. Apparently it heard me coming. Damn lucky I was looking where I was going. I moved uphill and it slid sideways, slinking down the slope.

Cold and scared, she entered the first night alone to find that she was living in a temple of great beauty.

How can I possibly sleep? It is so beautiful and exciting here. I'm snuggled in against the cliff in my high-up perch. I watched the mountains in the far distance turn soft-edged gray-pink. Dusk was soothing. I wondered if I'd be frightened, but instead am awestruck. The stars appeared so slowly, and I was trying to recognize the constellations when I realized that behind me was a very bright light. I turned to see the full moon appear over the deep black evening mountain.

During the night, the spirit of fear visited Natalie.

Last night I dreamed that I was in the middle of Death Valley, and I was in a phone booth. The phone rang and when I answered it, I said, "Hello, this is the wilderness."

Then I suddenly awoke knowing that something was moving on my head and hat. My hands started to jump toward my head to find out what it was, but fortunately the sleeping bag was constricting my movement, and I was awakened enough to *think*. "Be quiet, hold still, listen!" My heart was pounding. Adrenaline shot through my system. (This is one way to get warm, I said to myself.) As I stayed motionless I felt the movement on my head again. It seemed like scratching. My fear was that it was my friend the snake trying to join me in my sleeping bag to get warm.

After about ten minutes of wondering, listening, and moving slightly now and then, my panic subsided. I decided to move the top of my head out of the drawstring hole at the top of my bag. I could see clearly, in the moonlight, but did not see any animal. I pulled myself to a sitting position, still in the bag, to take a look around, being careful to move slowly. I saw nothing. By then I had figured it was a rodent; the scratching on my cap was so definitely a paw. It was obviously not a large creature or it would have made more noise moving. Figuring a rat wasn't going to do much damage to me if I let it be curious about my hat (thank god for the hat), I went to sleep.

Gradually she began to adjust to her surroundings and to sense the quality of the solitude to which she had come.

Listening to the silence is one of the most powerful and profound experiences I am having. At first I avoided listening. The lack of sound is so totally foreign, it is frightening to allow myself to become more aware of it. I can sit quietly awaiting the sunrise and — now that the wind is quiet — hear total nothingness except for my own breathing and the rustle of my movements, however slight. I will try to soak in that silence more completely later. It seems that I fear the letting go of myself into that total quiet, yet that's what I want to do.

What am I learning out here anyway? That I have tremendous inner strength and resources if left to myself and if I have a little luck and support. I don't get lonely when I'm alone. I am discovering that if I have a pen and drawing materials with me I don't need much more. I'm learning that I care enough to care for myself. That seems foolishly simple.

I am learning, somehow, about death. Although I have tremendous energy and excitement about living, the idea of dying – for me to become at one with the cosmos – does not frighten me. I find myself self-protective, but not out of death-fear as much as life-wish.

Nature was also giving her a name to match the strength and independence of her quest: Solo.

I saw three hawks soaring as I cried out to the sky, and watched the two pair off and leave together. The third (me) went on and on alone, higher and higher, and finally out of sight beyond the mountains. I cried as I saw that as the metaphor of me – yet I liked it.

On the evening of the third day she performed a ritual based on Black Elk's account of the *hanblecheyapi,* or "crying for a vision" ritual of the Oglala Sioux.

As I walked from the center position to each point on the compass, I moved slowly, with my eyes down, not focusing on anything. I concentrated on my breathing, being aware to breathe deeply with each slow step. When I reached the pole with the power object, I stood with my head raised to the sky and sang out my chant, loud and clear. It felt good inside to give full strength to my voice. It brought to the surface a lot of strong, indescribable emotions. I thought of my family. I appreciate them fully, without reservations, lovingly. When I stood in front of the objects on the south pole, I wept for love of my daughters. Being a mother of such fine persons is a great joy, forever, for me.

I thought of many other people I love. And I didn't think of anything. I lay down within my circle, for a time, I don't know how long. I was calm. Then I started moving around the ritual path again. When I got very cold, I left the circle quietly.

The next morning she returned to the others.

> I remember warm feelings of reunion. . . . Finally the sun gave us a
> break and warmed our bodies for our last afternoon united. We
> found ourselves sitting close together, talking rapidly of all our
> experiences, good and bad. After a while it was time to go. We
> packed up. The hike out was light and easy. I was in better physical
> shape than when we had arrived. My feet seemed to move across
> the rocky ground in the dusk with ease. . . .
> The moon was out again as we drove north on the eastern
> side of the Sierras. White, snow-capped mountains illuminated by
> the moon accompanied our pathway home. We turned off the road
> at a hot springs around midnight. The scene was like a Chinese
> scroll. Below us was a wide, quickly flowing hot stream. We took
> the winding path down the hill, hearing the gurgling and bubbling
> as we walked. The backdrop was high mountains in the distance
> with the moon watching over us. An arched bridge crossed the
> stream. Slowly, one by one, we undressed and slipped into the
> delicious water . . . our first in a week. So many beautiful people
> bathing in the warmth, the moonlight, the friendship. The steam
> from the river cast an unearthly air around us. Laughing and play-
> ing, quietly rejuvenating, I declared it was the most lovely Easter
> morning I'd ever seen.

MARK

The stories of vision questers do not always conclude with beatitude. It is not
rare for an individual to return early, before the three days and nights are over.
Those who do return early tend to feel that they have failed. This feeling of
failure may persist if the person is not helped to look clearly at the reasons for
returning. There are many good reasons. People sometimes go on a Vision
Quest when they might better employ their time facing some problem at
home. It might be difficult for a person to realize this, until she/he is alone
with a chance to reflect on the world left behind.

Mark, a popular and respected young high school teacher and counselor,
returned on the second night of his Vision Quest from high on a ridge in the

Panamint Mountains. He appeared at the edge of the campfire late at night, looking as if he had been wrestling with the devil. His first words were, "I feel like a failure." Subsequent scrutiny of his journal revealed that after an initial surge of happy feelings on the first day, he began to go back over recent events in his mind: the death of a close friend and the imminent deaths of his mother and father.

EVENING OF THE FIRST DAY.
After having my cup of tea, I thought, "What's next?" It didn't take long to figure that out. I thought of my friend Karl, who died on December 22, and I cried for at least half an hour. Then I cried for my dad, who is slowly dying in the liver and lungs, and my mother, who went into the hospital for cancer the night before I left on the trip. I didn't know if I was going to quit or not. I was scared. I was all alone, and that was more frightening than death.

I prayed to Karl for forgiveness in not seeing him in his final days. Would you believe I was scared to see him because I didn't want to cry in front of him? Just like dad. . . . After crying it out, I had another cup of tea, then prayed and meditated. I found myself with a lot of inner strength. I also did a small ritual with the fire. I gave and said small prayers to all the people on this trip with me, each and every member of my family, and my really close friends. Then I placed a solid piece of wood for all those friends and acquaintances I have known and worked with, partied with, had confrontations with. Then I stepped over to a high ridge and yelled out, HAPPY NEW YEAR, WORLD! and went to my sleeping bag, to sleep through the New Year, stone cold sober on that night for the first time in my life since age fifteen.

MORNING OF THE SECOND DAY.
God, how I am weak. I had to go down that friggin' mountain to build a few rocks for my partner, and I simply didn't want to. When I was halfway down, thoughts crossed my mind to give up, to say fuck it to the whole thing. Then came the thought that last night I was weak right before I started crying, and that after my cry I actually had a lot of strength. So I sat on a rock and cried for about a minute and pleaded with myself and the Lord not to give up. . . . I

just need to continue opening up with my heart and soon I will find strength.

I'm beginning to feel nauseous again. I'm also crying right now. I don't want to give up! My gut tells me to go back to base camp, but my *macho* tells me to stick with it. I don't know which one to give three cheers to. I just don't think I failed anything and yet I feel like a failure for just thinking about it. . . .

I have given my present situation some serious considera-tion. If I feel nauseous during the night or extremely weak in the morning, I'm going back to base camp, where I'm hoping to get hugs, because I sure need them.

He returned that night, hiking two miles back to base camp. We talked at length, until the moon was almost across the sky. We tried to help him see that the Vision Quest is not a matter of duration but of intensity, and that his feelings during the quest were an inner motion picture of his life in general. He began to talk with great affection of his mother and father. He also began to see why he had left his quest.

Why did I return? Fear of death and dying was the issue. I have been avoiding any mention of dying with my parents, and I have discovered that that has nearly brought about my own demise.

My present quest is the need to discuss this issue openly with my father and my mother. There is no doubt in my mind that I love them both dearly. I need them as much as they need me.

I need to focus on death and rebirth, to find out what it is that's so frightening. I find it easy to tell people that I fear death. It was something else, though, when I looked at death right in front of me. I confronted it internally for the first time in my life.

THE TWO SISTERS

Two Dominican sisters went with us into the Panamint Mountains to seek a vision. Teachers both, they were drawn by the idea through their love for the desert and the Biblical stories of Mt. Sinai and the prophets of old. In the two

80

of them the traditional and modern, the flesh and spirit, were blended in a special way. Listens With the Heart chose an alluvial terrace above Lost Springs Canyon, and the other, Ruth, went up Anvil Spring Canyon to the opening of Butte Valley.

As their journals reveal, each went about the quest in a different manner. Ruth, more traditional in her outlook, prayed for that which would bind her closer to God. ("Lord Jesus, I would like to be more ascetic . . . to be disciplined and to fast . . . to become closer to You in prayer.") The record of her three days and nights is filled with affirmations of faith and prayer and quotations from scripture. When she arrived at her place she climbed a mountain.

> I feel the need to see beyond my valley. . . . I am content and have no desire to check out other mountains, partly because of the realization that I have no food for further climbing. I thank God for such beauty and ask for His protection during my stay. I feel very secure with the gentleness of all the elements. I am not worried and know I have lots of time.

On the other hand, Listens With the Heart approached her quest with passionate, sensitive, self-critical energy.

> I washed and wrote up dreams and drew and felt yukky. Why did I come here? Yes, it's beautiful and quiet, but life is to be lived with people. People come into my thoughts and dreams. It seems meaningless right now to live without people and relationships. I am thinking of the quote, "It would be better for you to meditate in your own room. You are not ready to go out into the desert. You are still too attached to the world." I guess I had to come to find that out. . . . I find it hard to articulate why I wanted to come. Why have I come? To know God. I feel His presence, and it's so unemotional.

With her feelings of loneliness and doubt came also the cold winds of the night, to further test her.

> Cold — not wanting to be cold. Now the chills go through my body

and I watch them and don't tense up. And warmth follows. Can I let the chills from people go through me the same way and not tense up and allow the warmth – trust it – to follow? Will I?

For Ruth, the experience of the Vision Quest was one of innocent delight in little things. Having given her life over to God, she felt free to enjoy and experience without doubts or critical self-attention.

> My problems and worries have become as insignificant as sand shifting in the wind. Yes, I wish to seek a vision – a vision of Love. A Love that will free me to be really sensitive and caring. A Love for my God, greater than all loves. . . . To cry for Him with a desire yearning for nothing else. For with His Love all else is possible.

She went for a walk on her second day.

> As I turned toward the west I was surprised by a little rainbow. A rainbow in the evening sky in the desert – no clouds except where the sun was setting. I knelt down in gratitude. A rainbow is a special sign of hope and new life and joy. I decided to follow it.

As the sun set, she walked up the gradually opening canyon and was greeted by a bat and a jackrabbit. She picked a tiny branchlet of purplemat to leave for her buddy at the stonepile.

> My thoughts were going back to the others, hoping they also caught a glimpse of the rainbow. . . . I continued walking a little further, then stood still to see the sun slip down behind the hills. In my own way I gestured a prayer of thanks and then returned.

Listens With the Heart also saw the rainbow, but she followed it to her dreams, which were laden with archetypes illustrating inner conflict.

> An old Indian woman's face and a man came to me. There was a child in the cradle board. I took the child, to care for it alone. There was a stigma attached to it.

A red, yellow and white light appeared at the end of a black tunnel. There was a heavy silver chain suspended from a black iron fastening on the way {through the tunnel}.

I gave birth squatting. To twins, a boy first, then a girl. My love went more to the girl. The afterbirth came and . . . I put them {the children} in warm water after holding them against {my} skin.

Remarkably connected with her dreams, she was disturbed and fascinated. Her experience of the final night also shows strong intuitive and instinctive feelings regarding her life, her destiny and her deepest, innermost spiritual vitality.

When my circles were complete and I had brought in a sitting stone, I sat and waited for the moon to rise as she had the night before over the Mystical Mountain. She was slow in coming. I sat and waited until she was full over the peak. . . . She came forward like a host: "This is my body, given for your freedom."

My circles were ready. I was ready. But what to do? I did not know what to do. I, the prayer-teacher!

I began to walk around my circle and talk to the Lord. Did the Lord know I was there? In the vastness? Would He take time and be with me tonight? Now? Would He love me?

I wept in self-pity or from the pain of the cost of celibacy. And then I remembered all who have loved me in my lifetime. So many. I recalled them, place by place, where I had lived and gave thanks for them and prayed for them now — wherever they are — and my family, member by member.

I remembered an exercise about carrying a heavy rock as a reminder of the karma we carry. I chose a large one from the inner circle and held it in my arms and walked. It was heavy. I remembered my anger in my back and put the rock in my day pack and on my back and prayed for release of that anger.

Not only I carry karma. I prayed for the sick and lonely and disabled and divorced and alienated and mentally ill.

And the moon was halfway.

I sat in silence surrounded by my circle and by the ridges on both sides forming an earth womb with the mystical mountain at the opening to the northeast.

The giant mountain – the rock.

I wanted to take it into me.

The rock – a symbol of rebirth according to Jung. I do not understand.

I take it in and sleep takes me.

A friendly fly buzzes by to awaken me.

No dream. . . .

Then I hold the planet in my heart and wrap it in light and it is encircled by two gold rings moving around it. I remember my first dream: a warm, brown earth house in the desert. Out front, a sign: "Everybody welcome. Water and maps available." Maps to where? Inner journeying. Maps of consciousness.

The moon is three-fourths across the sky. I sit and wrap up in my sleeping bag. I build a fire. I bury it and sit on it and then sleep.

"Yaweh, I know you are near."

Two blue eyes look at me. Feminine eyes, teenage eyes. Loving, detached, inward, childlike.

I open my eyes. Morning has broken. A flash of lightning pierces a grave. Easter. Resurrection.

Alleluia, Alleluia, let the holy anthem rise
And the chorus of heaven chant it in the temple of the skies. . . .

Ruth reported her last night more simply. She did not feel the conflicting emotions felt by Listens With the Heart. She did not have to wrestle with the devil, or at least such a struggle with doubt and disillusionment is not recorded.

My last night at my place of vision was long. I prayed, thought of all those people I touched in some way. I prayed for them and our world today. As the night wore on I dozed off some. The moon stayed up all night.

I saw the sun rise. Beautiful red, reflecting off the mountains across the valley. It quietly swept the sky with colors like the Grand Canyon. . . .

The birds are beginning to wake up and sing their morning

song. I too will sing before my God.
> Sing a new song unto the Lord!
> Let your song be sung from mountains high.
> Sing a new song unto the Lord,
> Singing Alleluia!

On the last morning Listens With the Heart left her circle and her place with some difficulty. Although she had been very lonely, now that the time had come to be with the others she did not feel the pangs of separation from them as keenly. Her place had held her, taught her. Here she had become deeply connected to the earth.

> Time to get up and leave. I look at my circles and love my "home," the only home I ever built for myself. My tomb, my womb. I have to go. Reluctantly I pack up.
>
> I walk three times around my home. Father, Son, Spirit. I rededicate myself. I water the earth seven times as my gift and in thanksgiving. I linger. Perhaps I should wait for the orb of the sun to show? Procrastinating. Time to go. I put on my pack and deliberately step out. I survey my home with love and walk to meet my buddy. One more look. I wish I had a camera.
>
> Down at base camp I open Barbara's Tao book: "The longest journey begins with the first step."

Later, she reviewed her experience, applying the same rigorous, critical standards of self-appraisal she had used during her time of aloneness.

> The beginning of what? I had asked as I walked in circles. Trust. It will be good. No answers. No specifics.
>
> I was a bit resentful that it was only a first step, after so long. Later I rejoiced. A first step to whatever I have come for. I know it was a time of rebirth after so much death. Yes, it had happened.
>
> What?
>
> Nothing had happened.
>
> I didn't even stay awake all night.
>
> No dream. No vision.

Had I wasted the time? The opportunity?

Maybe. Vacillating between acceptance and disappointment?

Maybe if I'd known what I wanted? Had a clearer purpose?

Hours later in the car a flash came over me. I had reviewed the first one-half of my life. I was awed at what I had done. What had I done?

Hours later. Maybe I did too much? Did I listen? Was I passive enough? Did I allow space for the Other? No. Typical me, I talk, walk, do, and then fall asleep. . . .

The next night, tonight, my room is a mess—camping gear, Christmas, clothes, mail. Feeling closed in and like I have to hurry. So much to do. I'm almost shaking.

I have to meditate.

I sit on my bed, close my eyes and I am on my hill in my circle once again. Peace comes and expansion and light and letting go of muscular holding.

So this is why I went.

So I could be this now. Could I be this big under pressure? At school? Do I have to close my eyes and be alone?

Centered and expanded—both.

Ruth later described her Vision Quest in the same pure, simple terms that premise her life.

My experience of Nature is like a mother folding herself protectively and lovingly around her child.

Every rock, plant, cloud, sound and smell was kind to me. I felt safe, warm and peaceful. I tried to be very attentive to everything, listening with all my senses.

My visions were simple: the rib of a bird, shining, silvery rocks, the dancing bat, the rainbow around the sun, the frightened rabbit, burro prints, little flowering plants, quiet peace, the gentle wind and a strong awareness of friends, loving and caring.

O God, what more do I need than I have been led deeply into the very center of your love? Amen.

86

But Listen With the Heart was aware of something else. Her desert quest for a vision had troubled a deep well within her, the well of emptiness.

> Since I returned I have wanted to eat and eat and eat—and I have eaten a lot. But what do I want? It is not food/stomach hunger, really, although I attempt to alleviate it that way. What am I hungry for? What do I want?

Indeed, what *do* we want? How will we fill our hunger? The journal of every vision quester, in one way or another, has phrased this question.

CREOSOTE AND LOOKING INTO THE FIRE

A brother and his sister vision quested with us at different times over a five-year period. Each enacted the Vision Quest twice, on separate occasions. Each had an unsatisfactory first experience.

Creosote, a college teacher and divorced father of two, expressed interest in the Vision Quest at an early date, when the idea first began to take tentative form. Trained in intellectual and academic pursuits, he found the School of Nature to be in stark contrast to the ivory-towered life he led.

He went to Death Valley with a group of people from an alternative school and spent much of his time alone thinking about his children and his unhappy love affairs. He experienced no vision and had few insights that seemed notable to him. He did, however, have a near-fatal experience with the unfamiliar desert.

> This morning I decided to take a hike from where I was on the northwest topmost cliff above the canyon to the valley floor, which seemed a short stroll. I was thinking about my girlfriend and the fact that she was seeing another man, and I did not think about what I was doing. I thought a hike would lull my raging jealousy.
>
> When I finally reached the valley I realized that I had come too far, that I had overstepped my ability. Although I had drunk water before I started out, I did not have any with me. The day was hot. I lay down in the shadow of a rock and went to sleep.

When I awoke I was in full sun, and two ravens were circling over me. My throat was parched and dry. I felt dizzy and sick. I looked up to where I had come from. It seemed impossibly far away.

For a long time I just sat there and cried and felt panic. But the heat drove me to my feet, and I decided to try going back any-way. It was then I spied a shack, a half-mile away. It was an old miner's shack, seemingly abandoned some time ago, but the door was fastened tight. In my desperation I broke in. Inside, on a rough-hewn table, were two gallon water bottles. One was empty, the other was full. Beside them was a note: "This is good water. Please don't drink it all."

I don't have to emphasize how sweet that stale old water was. I might have died that day. I didn't, thanks to another human being with forethought.

I drank half a gallon of water and rested in the shade of the shack. Then I fastened the door as it was when I found it and walked back up to the top of the mountain.

Despite his experience, he was eager to try again, though he did not do so for nearly a year. In the meantime, he began to plug up some of the holes in his life's bucket. He began to see his children, whom he had not seen in some time, and settled down into a relationship with a woman who later became his wife.

His second Vision Quest, in the Last Chance Mountains in early April, was marked by terrible cold winds from the north, winds that took the legs out from under people, winds without mercy. Hoping to expand his awareness of the infinite, he was instead forced to come up with concrete, immediate answers to the question of survival. He found a place behind a low ridge to the leeward side of the wind and hung on, making brief forays to stretch his legs. In spite of the wind he wrote a great deal in his journal. At first, he was pleased with his situation. He enjoyed the opportunity to live in the third person of self-consciousness.

I adjust, make compromises, wait patiently, am impatient, exam-ine my myths about myself, discover beauty in barrenness of rock and rude, red soil, in cactus thorns and the hissing, yellow blos-soms of creosote, in blood from cuts in my hands, in the droppings of animals, the stainings of mineral, the precise artlessness of the way nature is arranged. I thrill to the morning sun breaking chill and clear on the wings of the North Wind. I find a belly flower in the bones of a dry wash. I feel my body in motion – it's hot and fluid, even in the cold. What a strange creature I am. I go to the edge of a cliff and gaze into the distance. Whatever, whoever I am, I'm alive.

Being with humans creates "time." Being alone in the wilderness creates a dimension other than time, a rhythm that is not in time. Time is a myth invented by people to mark their position in space relative to each other. But the other dimension, the rhythm that goes on and on, that is contacted only through the act of being *alone,* without the need to mark relative position – that is *eternity.*

On the second day he began to see things with a ritual eye.

I had been thinking about what it is that obscures my ability to take proper stock of my life situation. I was getting nowhere. Then I noticed an ant crawling up the side of my coffee cup. Absent-mindedly, I watched. I had nothing better to do.

The ant climbed to the rim of the cup and looked around, groping aimlessly with its antenna. Then it proceeded to crawl around the rim of the cup in a perfect circle, stopping where it had begun, where a tiny bead of moisture clung to the rim. As if by magic, three other ants appeared, attracted by the moisture and the gyrations of the other ant. Suddenly I was off, off on a flight of feeling and thought.

I can't say what it was all about. But I looked around at the dry, wind-swept desert and thought about water, the absolute importance of it, and how these ants knew that there was a little drop of water on my coffee cup. I spoke to them, told them I was pleased that they had found water, and promised that I would leave some water in my cup for their enjoyment.

The episode passed. I became aware again of the passage of time. But the rest of the day I found myself thinking about perfect circles.

On the third day depression took hold of Creosote. The insidious wind and the bleak landscape evoked a similar inner geography.

The wind blew all day, always from the north, with a steady, rending force that I could not resist. I screamed at it, cursed it, and finally accepted it. The chill fingers of the wind penetrated the micro-pores of my sleeping bag and the stones of my shelter wall. I spent the night in the grip of a strong, foreboding quasi-dream of disaster, of being consumed by the wind and cold. Toward morning something relented, said O.K. to the cold and the screeching of creosote in my ears. I went to sleep, only to awaken to another day of even higher winds.

I crouch against the shelter, my back to the wind. I can see across a ridge and down to the bleached bones of the valley. The terrain is bleak and uninviting. It is a metaphor for the way I feel about my life back there. Yes, there are a few cases, but generally things look pretty grim. I'm reminded of Antonioni's film, *The Red Desert,* and Eliot's poem, "The Wasteland."

Is that what I came out here to do? To contemplate the wastelands of Nature and to think black thoughts about what I'm going back to? What is my place in this wilderness world? What's it all about? Why am I here?

The prophet went into the wilderness and came back to the people crying, "Repent." I am no prophet. I am no saviour-god. I *am* one of those who need to repent. I confess. The abilities I possess have been used to gratify my own ego. Love? I have not learned how to love. Three wives later I am still trying to love people without hurting them, or manipulating them.

Why am I so bleak, so cold? Life seems absurd. "All life death does end, and each day dies with sleep" (G. M. Hopkins). I am afraid of death. I am more afraid of dying. I am sick of myself. I'll die like a coward. I'll live without love. Nobody will care. . . .

The wind continues to hiss in the creosote and thunders in my ears, and I hunch deeper into myself, into my misery of loneliness and self-pity. Everything around me, so ageless and enduring. What possible use my tears shed on this stony ground? Why, dear god, this stony ground?

I don't understand why I am so lonely. I didn't think I would miss people so much. The wind keening in my ears, the unresolved questions of my life lumped upon these rocks, in a sackful of flesh and bone. . . .

In a few more hours the sun will set on my last day here. The darkness will come on and I will wait for the morning light. . . . I must see the people among whom I live as those who have come to watch me die, even as I imagine them grouped around me now. I must walk among them as if I were a condemned man. But not as a stranger, or an outsider—as a fellow condemned human being. There is a kind of comfort in knowing that we all share this destiny. But what remains after we have given it all away? Whatever is left must be the way to live, to seek life.

I know I can grow and change and procreate and be astonished at myself and other people. I know that I can seek to live, somehow, in others, after my death. I can love individuals: my children, my ex-wife, my mother and father and sister and brothers and others of my family for being who they are, and, if I fiercely desire, I will love them beyond the grave.

I don't know what I can do about the rest of the world—the starving millions, the oppressed, the suffering innocents, and all those who seem to care for nothing but themselves. But I guess I can love as well as anybody and have faith that I can rise again like the wind and seek the branches of the creosote.

I'll try to stay alive and healthy and yearning to love, to put on new green leaves. And when I die my body can be used as fuel to keep somebody else warm—for a while.

The wind that carries the deadly snow is the wind that carries the seed. So my love shall thrive, even in the barren desert.

The stars are out tonight.

Looking up at them I experience the nausea of vertigo.

My body is getting older.

Slowly I am dying.

How terrible and how sweet:

The stars are out tonight.

Looking Into the Fire, Creosote's sister, also enacted the Vision Quest twice. Linked to her brother by blood and the shaping influences of a common family history, her experience points out similarities in the sheer persistence of their efforts to realize their vision. There are also differences between the two which contrast the cultural roles of male and female. Whereas Creosote more actively and aggressively pursued his vision, pinned down by the wind and fiercely desiring to find love, Looking Into the Fire sought vision by opening up, by becoming sensitive to the power and healing of Nature.

Looking Into the Fire had been living in Canada for three years on a lovely island in the British Columbian sea. But some part of her could not be happy. She became aware that she would have to leave her husband and the home she had helped build, and reenter the mainstream of civilization. At the suggestion of her brother, she appeared at our door looking for what she knew not. She volunteered to work with us for a while and became absorbed in the ongoing crises of our small, nonprofit corporation. Before long she found herself on a spur of Hunter Mountain (Panamint Range) surrounded by great slabs of granite and a forest of pinyon. It was hot and dry. Alone on her Vision Quest she went into a sharp depression reminiscent of her brother's experience in the Last Chance Range. She remembered her beloved island, the cries of the cormorants, the lapping of the waves. She cried for the memory of her home.

All I can think about are the mistakes I've made in my life; all the bad choices, or at least what feels like bad choices; all the manipulating I've done; all my big know-it-all-ness. I don't love myself. What a terrible thing to realize. All I can think of are times when I've spoken without thinking, times I've said things to impress others with my vast knowledge. Now I'm starting to cry, and it's self-pity. Poor me. I haven't learned how to take care of myself yet, nor do I know how to love. What a mess.

Great Spirit have mercy on me. I need to learn how to be silent. I need to learn how to love. I'm dirty, I'm tired, I'm hungry. I'm unhappy and I know nothing. Please show me how to live.

Later in the morning. . . . I finally got up, started my fire, and sat at the end of my sleeping bag to carve on a piece of sage – mainly cutting out the dead wood and exposing the new under the gray, weathered surface. I thought about myself and maybe this trip is symbolic of what I was doing to the piece of wood – cleaning out the dead and useless to see what kind of shape and texture is really underneath, which is me without all the trimmings I think I have needed all these years.

Wait, wait. I get so impatient. What is my name? I want a name so badly that big sobs form in my throat. Everything looks rare. Everything is in focus. The colors and brightness of objects jump out at me. I see faces, mouths especially, in all the rocks around me. Each one is heavy in deep repose. I search for beds, beds to sleep in, make love in, beds to die in. I would die by lying in the sun and have the sun slowly bake away my flesh to expose my bones. Then I would lie for years while the sun slowly bleached my bones to white and they were buried in the sand.

She stayed with us for six months and then declared herself eager to try the Vision Quest again. This time the knot of despair inside her was ready to come undone. She tested herself with questions. "Am I just hanging on to the past? Am I scared of the future? Can I really trust in my fate, in my karma, to see me through? Do I have good karma? These are words that don't say much. It's all in the *doing,* and I am afraid sometimes."

She found a huge, gnarled, half-dead Yellow fir beside a small stream high in the South Warner Wilderness and on the first night dreamed a dream.

I am standing at the edge of a huge chasm. There is a house at one end of the chasm—it is my house. I *have* to get to the other side. I could walk around, but for some reason this is not an option. Instead I take a long ladder and lower it over the cliff so that the top of the ladder reaches the other cliff—barely. I then start across the ladder on hands and knees, one rung at a time. I am afraid. I am trembling. I cannot see what is at the bottom, probably a stream, rushing fast over rocks. I cannot fall or I will die. As I am almost to the other side I slip and just in time grab a rung of the ladder. I am left dangling from the ladder, not knowing if I have enough strength to reach the other side.

The ladder was the link between her first quest and her second. Sleeping quietly through the night, she came to a new day and recorded heights of feeling and awareness that are the antithesis of her first quest.

I'm home! The stream sings in my body, flowing, flowing down through.

I am alone. I'm happy I'm alone. Maybe I can find in Nature some of the closeness, the unions my body craves. It is very dark now. The sky is immense and filled with stars. Please accept me, universe. I am just a tiny speck here, crouched over the fire by this stream flowing from this mountain I sit and lie on. The mountain is only a tiny speck. The Big Dipper has moved along the horizon. Oh, the stars! I'm thinking of those I love so dearly at home. I am grateful for those who have loved me and love me still. I love. I *can* love. I *do* love. If I can love then I must be a good person. I am a good person. Tomorrow I'm going to tell my tree friend who doesn't mind soaking up my tears in his dry hard skin.

I love this silence. The speaking is done by the wind in the trees, the birds who occasionally chatter, the buzzing of flies. We *need* the silence. It is in the silence that nature can speak to us.

Before she left her place, she had reached certain conclusions that were to affect her deeply and bring her back to us, balanced and certain within herself that she was ready to commit this time of her life to the work of Rites of Passage.

Bonded to the earth. Bonded. What good fortune led me to this place?

I asked the stream to give me a name as it seemed to be trying to say something. It said, "Looking Into the Fire." So I've been sitting here trying to figure it out. Maybe I'd better listen some more. . . . Now the stream says, "Vision, vision, vision. . . ."

Companion of the Wind, Fire Stick, Gift Bearer, Listens With the Heart, Sister Ruth, Creosote, Looking Into the Fire, Solo, Mark, we join our voices in reaching out to you. We have allowed you into the heart of our faith and despair. We are trying to Giveaway.

What we are trying to say is that we have experienced an ancient way of knowing, that we have endured, that we have listened to the silence, and that our loneliness makes us want to give.

Each of us, in our separate ways, faced an experience that was undeniably real. The events of the Vision Quest did happen. We watched the sun rise and set. We heaped stones. We found a place to exist, a place that knew us. The earth gave us signs, spoke to us with wisdom we could never quite fathom.

We were miserable, ecstatic, bored, anxious, afraid, brave, at peace. We believed in ourselves, found myths for ourselves. We doubted ourselves. We pitied ourselves, respected ourselves. We looked within and began to see. We saw ourselves within the cosmic scheme. Sometimes we felt insignificant. Sometimes we felt the universe within us. Sometimes we remembered death. Sometimes we sought to be reborn.

We climbed mountains and hugged trees. We sat in the sun and thought no thoughts. We tried to sleep, to still our racing minds, only to fall into dreams of ancient times. We poked our noses into holes and caves, unraveled the mystery of canyons and alluvial fans. Animals came to us and allowed themselves to be seen. Wildflowers pushed up through the dry wash of our eyes. In the shriveled, thirsty deserts we found springs.

Each in his or her own way learned how to endure loneliness, isolation, deprivation, fear and the silence. Each of us learned a secret something, a way to hold out through the darkness and the cold and the hunger of life. Each performed his or her own solitary ritual to prepare for, and to accept, the oncoming night. Some experienced "visions." Others did not. Regardless, we waited for the path to stand clear.

And then we were together again. We want to emphasize that because we were alone and starving we began to learn something about how to love. We are trying to say that it is not easy to love if you do not have the opportunity to be alone, cut off in the silence with your own cries ringing in your ears.

We returned to civilization, to routines, crises, schools, work, families, the clang and clutter of our suburban lives. Under the onslaught of the clock, we have all lost much of the memory of those vivid moments we spent alone with our creaking bones as the wind swept through our roofless, walless mansions of solitude. But what we remember is sacred beyond the telling. It was given to us by our Great Mother and will be ours until she takes us back into herself. What we will become is her secret. For now, she has given us back to life so that we can Giveaway. That is her part of the exchange, the gift of life.

And what is our gift to her, other than our bodies? What is our part in the sacred exchange? Are we worth nothing? Surely not. We make the earth fruitful with our consciousness.

So conscious of the play, the battles of the sun and wind. The sun's eternal pounding, warm and soothing, bringing death and life. The wind, sensual as it curves and flickers, sweeping down to mingle in the brittle dryness of this stone and the sturdy elasticity of the desert shrubs. My body changes in the desert dance of the elements. I become brown and lean. Then my weakness overwhelms me and I am ash in the sun's path. The earth will retrieve me. I become mulch craved for a single creosote. We are born wet, fresh, and die bones.

I feel that nothing can blow away but the core of me. Nothing can be lost but my life. I feel solid and smooth and precariously balanced. A speck of pollen in the wind.

−Lonely Heart Outreaching

BOOK 4

4. THE MYTH

. . . for the problem is nothing if not that of render-
ing the modern world spiritually significant . . .
nothing if not that of making it possible for men and
women to come to full human maturity through the
conditions of contemporary life.
—Joseph Campbell, Hero With a Thousand Faces

Before we ever go into the wilderness to enact the Vision Quest, we talk
about myth. The Vision Quest takes life, concentrates it into a brief span of
symbolic time, and marks it into three basic processes: the severance (birth),
the threshold (life), and the reincorporation (death). These processes may be
reversed: severance (death), the threshold (passage through death), and
reincorporation (birth).

From this basic dynamic unfold all the myths of the world, told and
untold. The dynamic itself is mythical and is the source of the "mono-myth," or
archetypal myth, that underlies all myths. The plot of this myth goes as
follows:

And then the hero/ine left everything behind, forsaking the mother, the
world and all that was dear, and went alone and apart to a sacred, magic place
where was contained a secret, a treasure, a key to transformation of self and
the world. There, in that sacred place in the body of the Great Mother, the
hero/ine is tried by God or the gods, or the Great Spirit, and faces the

monsters of her/his karma. Through a long, dark night of the soul, the seeker waits for guidance in the form of wisdom or strength. Persevering, the quester is rewarded. She/he is revived, reborn, the inner eyes are opened, a vision is perceived. But now the main condition of the vision is that the protagonist return to the mortal world with the gift of vision, seeking to sustain and regenerate the world.

Such is the basic mythical foundation of the Vision Quest. Likewise, the modern hero/ine leaves the world behind and goes off to a place alone and apart. There, this modern protagonist is tried by the Great Mother and faces the dragons of karma. Through the long, dark nights the hero/ine waits for the visionary gleam. Carrying the burden and the gift of this new insight, the hero/ine must then return to the mortal world and seek to revive it from its death.

In this correspondence between the mono-myth and the Vision Quest lies the essence of the therapeutic formula that underlies every Vision Quest experience: "As in the rite of passage, so in life." The mono-myth is not only the basic myth of the Vision Quest; it is the basic myth of life. The Vision Quest merely provides the chance for modern individuals (no, not individuals, but heroines and heroes) to live this plot in a formally marked and guided situation, matching their sense of who they are against the archetypal motifs of the mono-myth.

It occurred to me as I awoke and crept out of the warmth of my sleeping bag that all of life is like a Vision Quest solo. That is why I have always held to the secret knowledge of the beauty and desirability of death – why I yearn, now that my task is nearing completion, for the end of it and the return Home, to comfort and peace. We came into this life as we went out on Vision Quest – not to have fun or be happy. We even anticipated dangers, discomforts, challenges, unpleasant sensations. Yet we came for the vision and to learn, to grow, to change, to evolve. Surely, there are joys in life as there are moments of both insight and delight in the desert we have chosen for our quest; but the experience here is only embroidered with joys; the basic material on which the delightful designs are worked is Trial that borders on sheer survival. So it is with a life.

I will be glad to return to camp and have something to eat after my fast. I will be glad to return home to take a bath, get the

grime out of my hair. So it is with death. The return Home. To rest. Then to use what we have learned in this life for the purposes beyond our present imagination at levels of consciousness we can only dream of. Thus to die well is to live well so that the maximum learning can be taken Home to our people.
—Gift Bearer

It has often been said that our modern world lacks mythical meaning, that people no longer see themselves as heroes and heroines. This has not been true in our experience. Those who were willing to place themselves in the self-conscious position of enacting the role of mythical protagonist in a rite of passage discovered how easy it was to assume that role.

In their journals and in their behavior the vision questers describe themselves. They left everything behind. They faced the dragon in the wilderness place. They caught a glimpse of the visionary treasure. They returned with their gifts to give away, their seeds to sow. In their stories are found the motifs of the mono-myth.

As we read the journal accounts of those who quest for a vision, we observe that these people are engaged in the making of myth. They are making a language of words and behavior that is their own unique expression of the Urge To Be. As this urge is ultimately inexpressible, myth is the only tool by which it can be measured.

The following accounts are to be read as modern variations on the ancient mythic theme of severance, threshold and reincorporation. Some of the accounts are written in the first person; others are written in the third person. All are illustrative of the way in which people of the contemporary world are able to render their world spiritually significant, through their actions, by their words, within the mono-mythic dimensions of participation in the Vision Quest. All are illustrative of the need within our modern culture to involve people in forms of behavior that reveal the full potential of the collective gift to make myth a gift by which people transform themselves and the world around them.

You Must Leave Everything Behind

Little lamb, who made thee?
Dost thou know who made thee?
—William Blake, "Songs of Innocence"

Having ventured forth across the threshold of birth, the child is cut from the mother. This necessary physical act of severing the umbilical cord, of separating the child from the oneness that was before, is merely the first step toward preparing the hero/ine for the time when she/he must again be severed from the mother world. This mother world, from which the hero/ine must be severed for a second time, is, or is like, the peacefulness and security of childhood. It is attached to the protagonist through a variety of umbilicals, or life-support systems. The heroic journey of the life-quester does not begin until the individual is strong enough and ready to cut the umbilicals voluntarily.

The mother herself plays a leading role in preparing her child for the heroic journey. This role is complex and demanding, and requires that the mother love the child, knowing that the child must leave her. The mother must also trust the inherent destiny of the child, for ultimately that trust will be tested by the reality of separation.

In a variant of the mono-myth, the mother is killed by her offspring, so that the heroic journey may begin. That is to say, the maternal ties that bind the hero/ine to the mortal world are removed. The hero/ine must stand alone at the threshold of birth. This birth is like a death and is, in fact, a symbolic enactment of the ultimate act of physical death.

From this paradox of symbolic birth and death comes the following account. My wife, vision questing with our nursing, eight-month-old daughter, describes the nature of the maternal influence and the richness of its impartation. The child, Selene, became sick with the croup. The weather turned bad. Mother and sick child lived for three days together in the Inyo Mountain wilderness, far from the support systems of civilization, in an

102

archetypal relationship that recalls the experiences of mothers throughout human history. Within the account of this experience are found the seeds of the child's eventual severance from the mother and the mother world, perhaps most clearly expressed in the mother's wish that Selene, for the moment, did not exist, and in her trust that our child was strong enough to survive the crisis.

There are two archetypal tales of severance contained in this account. One is told by the mother, who, like the Great Mother, nurtures, teaches, and protects her young, living to enrich and strengthen them to survive the ordeal of life. The other story is told by Selene, who, having been born, must now begin to prepare for eventual separation from the mother and for the heroic journey.

MEREDITH AND SELENE

JANUARY 8. EVENING.

The hills are quiet, eternal rock. The sun slowly laps across the valley, flaming pale orange on the hills. And only this vastness calls comfort, striated in color. The peeling dust of the mountains erodes my feet; the taste is dry. All I want is for Selene to sleep, and for me to have time to think. I want the night to pass.

I'm scared that she'll wake up choking. Right now I wish there were no such being as Selene, that I never knew the slightest taste of the devastating love she has awakened in me. I wish it were Steven and I, no third, no worry but ourselves, no tentative breathing that even now cracks as she breathes. But here she lies, asleep, beside the fire.

I'm restless, can't possibly imagine sleeping. I look to the mountains and they are too stern, too eternal . . . never having felt the split of heart over a small child who is sick.

Oh Steven, I long for you. Pray god that she sleeps the night through.

Great Spirit, have mercy on me,
For I am alone and ache for my child.

JANUARY 9. MORNING

Because I had imagined a long, hard night, each breath she drew

103

seemed strained, hinted in rasps next to my ear, and my adrenaline shot sharp flashes through my body, rotting my stomach, banishing the tiredness. But slowly the tiredness soothed my fears, her breathing calmed, and I slept, knowing I'd all too thoroughly thought of the worst possibilities and considered what I would do in each case. Throughout the night we shifted in the dark, pressed tight, and though her ragged breathing grew worse, it never reached choking, but only became a hoarseness that calmed at my quiet words to her. My milk flowed, no doubt from maternal urgency.

The sun rose splendid. The clouds eternally sweep across the sky. What will today and tonight bring? Was that a whistle far up the canyon?

Are those rain clouds? They seem to be moving to the higher mountains, to be broken into snow. I'll keep the fire stoked, wait, keep Selene quiet, though she's anxious to roam. Her throat rasps at each breath, but she eats well and seems to be as full of smiles as ever. If she'll sleep once more I'll let her loose.

Walked up Paiute Canyon with Selene on my back, drawn toward Steven. It was the only way Selene would sleep, finally. Now she lies in the sleeping bag, coughing every so often, roughly. I feel confident and strong when I walk.

How I love the quiet. I confused the rush of atoms in my ears with the hope of footfalls. Time has no relevance for me today . . . only the watching of signs in Selene, and the threads of sound and movement. . . .

Now we have returned from Willow Creek spring, a mile or so away. On leaving she cried, feeling sick and restless. She had awakened from her nap feeling worse, rasping. She ate a little, drank a little, and wanted to be held quietly a lot. So as she began to cry in the backpack I took her out and held her again for a while, and she fell asleep. I enjoyed the walk, keeping a strong, steady pace and watching the small movements of silence. Bird, sagebrush flicker, dust, sky-clouds, a burro, a willow branch, track shadows on the parched wash. For the first time I *see* how mountains erode. . . .

I see the sun break through the clouds above where others in the group must be. Down here the mountains shade the sun,

passing only shafts of light. I miss the group, watching them discover. To be sitting, listening by the fire, with my man at my side.

JANUARY 10. MORNING.

Up again before the chill dawn. Selene hacks more than ever, but
still she is good-natured. After I bundle her in the sleeping bag,
build a fire, and feed her orange pieces for her dry throat, her ragged
breath quiets.

Dust, the matting of dust everywhere – in every crack,
seam, hair, pore.

The clouds thicken up the canyon. The peaks are shrouded
in foggy cloud. More seems on its way. Snow? Perhaps. I'll keep a
fire going. Must get more wood. I continue to have a difficult time
eating.

My milk is intermittent, like the stream winding its way
down Paiute Canyon.

Just went and got two more gallons of water from Willow
Spring and collected screwbeans (mesquite). Now drops of rain are
falling.

AFTERNOON

Selene is asleep, but restless. Very overcast. My eyes keep wandering to the sky. I walk up to the top of this gulch searching for the
direction or intent of the dark clouds. The valley is beautiful. The
sun's rays slant down to the salt lake.

I feel at one with all the mothers through the past ages who
had no doctors and were exposed to earth's elements. My concerns
are: trying to keep Selene quiet or sleeping; gathering more wood
(we must stay warm); looking up, around, always to the sky, trying
to see where the storm moves; feeling my breasts (do I have enough
milk? the only thing that can provide her antibodies now). The
weather is deteriorating. I must keep drinking water. So hard to
eat. Feel sick at trying – though overall I feel healthy, dirty, dusty
and strong.

Sometimes, maternal preparation for severance is incomplete. The heroic act
of setting forth alone and freed from the mother ends prematurely. An individual
may match her/his ability against the terms of the mono-myth only to

discover that she/he has aimed too high, at least for the time being. The first step often proves to be the most difficult. Failure to take the first step into the threshold of the heroic passage does not indicate a lack of heroism. For many who have been ill-equipped by the maternal world, even spending a few brief hours away from that world is a heroic act.

Lucy, a sixteen-year-old girl, with an overprotective mother who nevertheless was anxious that her child become self-reliant, went with us into the desert to Vision Quest. There had been some question about Lucy's ability to live alone in the harsh land of cactus and stone. But she was resolved, though a bit naively, to go through with it and had obtained permission also from her doctor, who noted that she was subject to *petit mal* seizures.

Accompanying a group into the mountains east of the Saline Valley, she encountered severe winds and a bleak landscape utterly foreign to her. The night before the morning of the threshold, she exhibited obvious signs of fear. Obviously, her fear was genuine, deeply felt, as only a heroine might feel. The next morning I left her at her place. She said an apprehensive goodbye. For the next three days I would be her buddy. The following is from my journal.

Lucy

Some time during the first night I was awakened. Someone was shining a light in my eyes. Then I realized I was lying on my back and the full moon was in my face. The fire was out. The wind whipped through the ashes. I tried to take a drink from the water bottle. It was frozen. I threw more creosote on the ashes and relit the fire. Everywhere the quicksilver of the moon. For an hour or so I sat by the fire.

The wind sat up with me, passing through the upper air like an invisible horde, scattering the silence into crystals of raw sound, pounding my body into gusts. Day was breaking on the teeth of the wind.

I placed my bottle near the fire, to thaw it out. I wished I had mittens and a warmer coat. It was Good Friday.

I had awakened because I had been dreaming about Lucy. Now a premonition that all was not well permeated my cold, cramped world.

Reluctantly I said goodbye to the tiny solace of my fire and its cave of

106

attention. I bundled up and went into the kingdom of the wind, looking for a girl named Lucy.

Half an hour later I found her pack. Its contents were scattered and blown in the wind. Kleenex and clothing plastered the mesquite. I picked up a comic book that was caught in a claw of desert holly: *Horror Comics*.

For a long time I just stood there, looking into the maze of the mountains. I called her name into the wind. There was no answer.

Up the wash was a tiny fresh water spring that had been used for thousands of years by people migrating west into the Inyo Mountains, looking for rabbits and pinyon nuts. Before crossing the great valley to the upper slopes of the mountains, they had lingered here.

As the girl had expressed fears about being alone for seventy-two hours, we agreed that she would keep her vigil here, near the spring, where I would stop by each day. I said the spring was a friendly place, that many people had camped here with gratitude and happiness. She seemed to accept the positive side.

But something had obviously gone wrong. For some reason she had left this place of security. I wondered if I should contact the others and organize a search party or if I should continue on my own for a while. I decided to look for her, reasoning that if I increased my altitude I might see her.

Imagine a human being as seen from the unblinking yellow eyes of a raven riding motionlessly on the wind. From a thousand feet high there is not much to be seen. A dark speck changes direction, climbs out of a canyon and takes to the ridge. From this height the motions of the speck seem aimless, random. There is no emotion, only pure motion: distance covered and time taken to cover it. From the raven's point of view, hanging on its invisible strings of air, nothing is amiss, except that now there are two specks, one which is moving and one which it has been watching for some time and might have a hankering to eat after a while.

The moving speck winds along a south-tending ridge. It stops and looks down. It sees her, somewhat below and to the west. It was a long time before she was able to recognize my presence. When finally she calmed, she said she wanted to go home to her mother. The raven circled above the two human forms crouched in their world of fear and love.

Lucy had listened too intently to the night wind and had heard the voices of dead Indian souls who hovered around the spring. And then she saw them, fierce, proud, alien people, and she cried for her mother to help her but her mother was 500 miles away. Panicked, she went into the night in search of her buddy. Failing to find him, she succumbed to terror as the sun rose.

The wind howled out of the north, like death, ever present, colder than the gaunt, black bird that hung upon it. And the earth turned on her axis and the sun dawned in a cloudless desert sky. On the cold, red rock deserts of Mars the thin wind seethed, and the sun, a small, dully-glowing ball, drifted across the whistling sky. In the ammonia-methane wastes of Jupiter the wind congealed into the ultramarine clouds of liquid, poisonous atmosphere, as the sun, a large star, drifted across the skies of purple and yellow. On the frozen inertness of Pluto the wind did not blow and the sun did not shine and the heavens were eternal night.

And into the wind Lucy cried, "I want my mother." The wind muttered and moaned at the gravel beneath her feet. Lucy called again, "I want my mother!" and again the wind replied, only this time its language could be understood. The wind said, "Here I am."

You Must Go to a Place Apart and Sacred to Nature.

The eyes of fire, the nostrils of air, the mouth
of water, the beard of earth.
— William Blake, Proverbs of Hell

The hero/ine severs the ties to the maternal world and steps alone across the threshold into the sacred world of Nature. In this world, the wind and the stars, the stones and weeds, the sun and waters are symbols of regeneration. In this world the terms of life and death are clearly defined: the Great Mother gives and the Great Mother takes away. Hers is the testing ground, the arena, upon which the quest is staged. Symbolically, the world of the Great Mother is a grave, or a womb, wherein the hero/ine dies and is reborn.

In this sacred place there is a mutual exchange between the body and the environment, occasioned by the solitude and emptiness of fasting. The object of hunger, the food desired, is the body of the Great Mother herself, which is given sacramentally. That which is desired by the Great Mother and given by the quester is the body: flesh, urine, dung, spit, sweat, semen, secretions, breath and words. This stuff given to Nature is the same stuff that, in archaic myth, God infuses with divine life.

In the following account, a young man from Marin County, with no formal training in the self-generation of ritual, celebrates his union with the Great Mother. The stuff of the earth is arranged by his consciousness into a meaningful, dynamic configuration of death and rebirth. The location is *la bahia de la concepcion,* Baja California Sur.

BROKEN HEART LAUGHING

After waking and preparing this morning, I was given a sign: a prairie falcon flew south along the water and dove in that direction. It was the way I had decided to go last night. On the shore I lifted up a piece of driftwood. Underneath was a mouse who told me this was the land of innocence and understanding. A butterfly said: walk lightly, not heavily.

I sang prayers of thanks as I walked along. When I came to a large tree by the edge of the road I stopped, sat down and put my hands over my eyes and stared into the darkness. Soon a red light appeared, then it took on more shape and seemed like a heart artery. The shape was round and had little threads on it. The middle would change shapes and colors. Then it changed to bright blue and white and changed shapes, growing large, then shrinking. In the core I seemed to see shapes of the desert, big cardone cactus and the mountains. Suddenly I heard a noise that sounded like a car coming down the road. I opened my eyes quickly and still saw the blue-white light. It was so strong that the cactus and the road surrounding me were hard to see. I walked down the road staring at the ground and the white light which veiled its detail. After a minute the light disappeared and things returned to normal. . . .

Found the right spot for the circle. A butterfly showed me where to build it so I started building it four stones at a time – to represent the four corners of the earth. The circle is almost completed. I only left a space through which to enter it. I think I will also put sand on the bottom of it. One thing I didn't notice until it was almost done was that it is right next to a red ant hill. A voice told me it would be O.K. anyway. I imagined the circle being my womb and tomb.

A butterfly told me I already have much of the power I ask the Great Spirit for. Raven said so, too, when I thought of it again. What I really seek is understanding. . . .

Walked into the circle through the opening I had left for that purpose. Placed my sleeping bag and pad in the middle and went through everything in the bag and my possessions to make sure everything needed was there. It was.

Next, the five remaining stones needed to close the circle came out of the bag and took their positions. The circle was complete. Prayers and songs symbolizing this completion came forth.

Next, the four directions represented by a black lava rock (west), a white oyster shell (north), a yellow clam shell (east), and a red rock (south) were positioned. I sang to each of the directions as they appeared within the circle.

A sacred herb found a resting spot on each of the directions, and I asked it for its healing power so that my people may live. Then I sang a prayer to the One who is all the directions for strength and wisdom and understanding that my people may live. I cried loud and long, then sat down and wrote a little.

Soon, it seemed right to put my pen down and watch the last brightness of the day be engulfed by the night. I sang more and prayed more. Loud was my cry in the desert wilderness. For three days I had lived in it alone spending most of my time under a bush home, and now, enclosed by a universal circle, it was culminating.

I listened to the voices of the night and the rustling of creatures close by. Thoughts of loved ones, work and destiny filled my head.

Later, the night found me upon my back. It was time for lamentation. Personal and world events doused in sorrow and pain welled up from my stomach. Each one was released by a mournful cry toward the starry heavens. Cries arose from my plexus and were uttered forth with a loud wail. This continued for about one-half hour. Then I was finished and felt the surging power of life pulse within my middle.

The stars moved above me. Coyotes sang to me and reminded me to stay awake. Flute pranced out of its green house and was offered as a gift to the great one. Many of the notes reverberated in secret places inside of me. A few birds added their own melodies to the gift song. Cardone cactus stood still and tall on the perimeters of my circle, silhouetted by the starry sky.

The vigil was growing longer. I stared at the seal skull and thought of my body's eventual death. Will the part of me that cries and listens also die? Or does it remain a conscious pulse in the universal life? Only death holds the answer to these questions for me. But in the night I imagined the seal skull disintegrating and becoming soil for new life. And the green seed pod—it must turn brown and die before the life within it can spring forth.

More singing of prayers; one asking for strength to heal, another for understanding. The night, by this point, seems endless. Star companions moved all the way from the eastern horizon toward the western one, then they turned and traveled north. I long for the sunrise and search the east for the slightest sign. The blue-black sky framing the red eastern mountains has turned half a shade lighter. I wonder if it is just the moon. But the shade stays and not even a sliver of moon appears. The light-dark spot grows larger; it seems certain now that it is the sun. I make prayer and song to it as the giver of life to all living things. Behold, the warmer of the earth!

The light shade grows lighter and creeps further along the eastern horizon, both to the north and to the south. Rising to my feet I absorb it. I feel wide awake and very alive. My heart pounds in my chest, soft muscle sends hot blood coursing through my veins. Orion fades as the red sky races north and south over the mountains, then jumps over my head and caresses the western range beyond the bay. Many birds have joined my salutation. I see them dart through the brush on their first flight of the day.

All my gear is placed outside the circle. I shed my cotton skin and stand in the circle which represents both my womb and tomb. Skull and seed pod are nestled at my feet.

The eastern peaks glow red and soon the sun warms my chilled body. Loudly I sing my last prayers for strength, understanding and peace. I feel as if I already have many of the gifts I ask for. The day has come. The earth has once again been reborn in the greenness of life.

Skull points east from the center of the circle. I form a cross in the sand stretching to the four directions. Seed pod clutched in hand I am ready to go. The boundary is crossed.

Seed pod finds a new home in the bank of the wash and is encouraged with voice to continue. I sing to the mountains and my fellow questers as I travel north across the salt flat toward base camp. A joyous vision appears at the edge of the salt flat: my buddy Anthony is walking towards me. My heart soars, and soon we embrace. We leave our rock pile standing and walk toward camp together.

In the threshold place of the Vision Quest, symbolic death and rebirth take the form of actual entry into the body of the Great Mother, being reborn through a kind of regenerative incest with the things of the earth. Shorn of the past, the hero/ine descends into the abyss, into the sea, the pit, the belly of the whale, the dark cave, seeking the spark of identity, regeneration, and vision.

Wandering in a wash at the foot of the Dry Mountains, a vision quester found a natural equivalent to the heroic passageway in the body of the Great Mother. Entering, he reenacted the mythical womb-death and came forth with new insight.

ROCK

Last night while exploring just before dark I discovered a power hole, where I am sitting right now. The power hole is a natural hole in the top of a rather hard, volcanic-like, glass rock. The hole drops straight down about four and a half feet. The opening is egg-shaped and just large enough for a person's shoulders to slip through. I am now sitting in and absorbing the power generated by this hole. . . . There is a faint trickle of water that I use as a mantra. Of course it is completely dry in here, so there must be an underground stream within ten feet of the inner walls.

The walls of this small and magical place are ornate and detailed. There are thousands of small holes and caverns that form patterns of color and texture, each one with a history and story of its own. It's interesting to think how these little holes took hundreds of years in their development and yet find themselves all collected together in the same place at the same time – like people surprised to find themselves alive in the same era as their friends and lovers.

Had I been hiking around trying to reach some destination on the horizon I would never have bothered to spend several hours in this damn hole. I shall return tomorrow for more of the hole's wisdom. . . .

I must create my own myth with me as the center. Whenever I notice myself giving people the right to judge me or watching myself through their eyes, I must tell myself that I need to depend

113

on only me to derive security. The more I seek the approval of others, the less secure I will ultimately be. I see myself as a beautiful rock in the desert among thousands of other rocks. While the actions of certain rocks will affect the position of nearby rocks, no one rock is seeking the approval or guidance of any other. Rocks don't really need other rocks. It just happens that they usually are together, like in this wash.

My mission is to be me and to attain this by exerting as much effort and worry about who I am as these rocks do. My myth is a rock. All the rocks around me are as beautiful as I am. How could a rock ever wonder if he is a rock? Well, I asked all the rocks around the creosote tree how they got so confident.

"Rocks, how come you're so confident?"

"Because I'm a rock, just a beautiful rock."

"Rocks, tell me what it is all about, please."

"Because I'm a rock, just a beautiful rock."

"Rocks, how come you don't fight and quarrel and try to impress each other?"

"Because I'm a rock, just a beautiful rock."

"Rocks, you must make love a lot because there are so many of you."

"Because I'm a rock, just a beautiful rock."

"Rocks, I want to be a rock too."

"You are a rock, just a beautiful rock."

The sun is long gone and I am keeping watch over the fire. Yes I am hungry, but not very. I will tend the fire as long as my eyes stay open.

I've taken L.S.D.

I've taken E.S.T.

I've taken Mind Dynamics.

I've tried Jesus Christ.

I've read Perls, Rogers, Jung, Maharishi, Meher Baba.

I've driven fast.

I've been to bed with beautiful women.

I've come close to death.

I've been in jail.

I've been stoned years at a time.

I've met criminals, millionaires, geniuses, musicians.
I've been loved and I've loved.
I've traveled a little.
I've had quasi-mystical experiences and fantastic psychological insights.
I've been a hero.
I've been a bum.
And none of these things has ever changed me drastically.
And all of these things have changed me a little.
I am a rock.
I don't need to change.
I only need to experience whatever comes up.
The search is over.
I AM, and I'll probably forget that I AM.
But I know now that seeking change is the best way to avoid being beautiful.
I AM.
I AM a rock, just a beautiful rock.

Here You Must Be Tried. You Must Face the Dragon.

Tyger! Tyger! burning bright
In the forests of the night,
What immortal hand or eye
Could frame thy fearful symmetry?
—William Blake, "Songs of Experience"

The heroic passage is a road of trials. Separated, alone, given over to the Great Mother, the hero/ine enters the fearful darkness and confronts the naked self, the apparitions and shadows of the mortal state of being. Here the solitary battles against the inevitable monsters must be fought.

The hero/ine does not court fear; but fear must be faced. The treasure of the quest cannot be found without enduring the despair of ever finding it. The trials of the heroic passage exist because strength and courage exist, but these traits are found only in combination with vulnerability and fear.

In the following account a young woman, alone in the vicinity of Starvation Canyon, Death Valley, succumbs to fear, only to encounter an even more fearful situation brought about by her own decision to retreat. Her response is heroic in the mythical sense and demonstrates that the ability to be heroic has not been lost.

TRISHA

The plan was that after we found and established our power places, we'd meet back at the stonepile and from there we would all go to everyone's spot to get a good idea of where they were. As it turned out, we were damned lucky to be so efficient in our plans.

When I first found my place, before returning to the stonepile, I was filled with apprehension and wondered what the hell

I was doing in the middle of the desert by myself. I was so upset I actually started crying. Bill, who was on his way back down to the stonepile, found me, and I told him my fears. He was so nice, he offered me the choice of going to his camp with him. I told him no, because I didn't want to ruin his Vision Quest. Then he suggested that I try to stay out one night, and he would be in to check on me in the morning. That really made me feel better and I was determined to give it a try. Then we went back to the stonepile where Laura [a third buddy] was waiting.

After returning from the stonepile and my other buddies' places, I figured I better set up my tarp in order to keep out of the sun. I did and got myself situated underneath the tarp with my journal. I proceeded to spend the whole day there – almost.

As the hours passed I was getting more and more fearful of the thought of spending three days and nights alone. People who aren't in that position can't fully understand what I mean. Even now, trying to recall those feelings is really difficult. I don't feel I can describe them.

Anyway, this big, dark cloud almost covering the whole valley was overhead. The next thing I knew I was involved in the biggest, loudest, longest clap of thunder I've ever heard in my life. That's when I decided I needed to go to base camp. The simple truth (but it's not simple at all) was that I needed people, even one person. There was another clap of thunder and that set me to shaking, trembling.

I packed up as quick as I could, not even stopping to untie the string on the tarp – I cut it with my knife. . . . As I was walking toward Laura's place I remember thinking just an insignificant thought: "Oh, I'll go see how Laura's doing."

When I reached her she was sitting (or trying to sit) near a creosote, on her jacket, without a tarp for shade. It was literally impossible for her to lift her head by herself, and mucus was pouring out of her nose onto her shoulder and it filled her mouth. I tried to calm her, although I was not feeling well. Actually I think seeing her in that state made me grab hold of myself and realize that her safety was my responsibility. I tried real hard to do anything to help her, but everything I suggested to her brought the replies, "In a

117

minute," "This is an emergency, help me sit up," "Help me lift my head," or "I want to lie down."

After talking to her for what seemed like forever, I finally got her to realize that I had to leave to go get help, that we needed help. I promised her I'd be back in fifteen minutes with Bill and that he would help us (she didn't even know who Bill was). . . . By this time I was really feeling ill, while at the same time feeling that I had to run to get Bill. I was afflicted with the dry heaves a couple of times. Finally I started puking water and yellow liquid. I had to lay down twice to clear my head, saying, "Everything is going to be O.K. You're doing fine. No more barfing, O.K.?" I reached my spot and realized that Bill was not too far away. I commenced yelling his name as loud as I could. While I waited for him, I figured out a cry and started saying it over and over again: "Great Spirit, I am in fear for my friend's life and mine. Please help us."

When Bill and I reached Laura she was still incoherent. She asked us where she was and what she was doing here. We answered her, and it seemed she realized what was happening, because she said, "Oh yeah, solo." Bill then left for base camp. He said he would return in about an hour. We waited. It began to get dark, and I started to get worried, even though in the back of my mind I knew that they would find us. I made a fire pit and was on my way to gather wood when I heard voices. I thanked the Great Spirit.

The dragons of the threshold are real. Pains and fears come, and there is no one else to help. Whatever comes must be faced alone. The hero/ine recognizes this and, for the sake of future fulfillment, in the name of humanity, endures the dark night.

Yet the trials of the Vision Quest are like the everyday trials of life, battles with loneliness, depression and self-doubt. Battle with dragons such as these is absolutely necessary if the hero/ine is to attain, "Death of the self in a long, tearless night, All natural shapes blazing unnatural light" (Theodore Roethke, "In a Dark Time").

In all little deaths the ultimate death is reflected. Above all, the hero/ine respects this ultimate death and so lives with reverence and tenacity

118

in the company of dragons who symbolize this death. Those who endure are not necessarily the strongest or the best prepared. Those who endure will be those who have learned to live with their weakness. Thus the hero/ine allows her/himself to *be,* to be weak, to be strong, and to face the dragons whose mother is death.

The story of Liz illustrates the kind of monsters that the hero/ines of the Vision Quest must often face. They are alone, without help, too proud to retreat, in despair of going on. The situation they face is one for which their secure childhood never prepared them. What is it that makes the hero/ine go on, in the cold, without a fire, to the warmth of a new day? What follows is from my journal.

Liz

Liz said she knew how to start a fire. "With wet wood?" I asked. "No, show me." So I showed her how to use the inside bark of sagebrush and peelings from juniper. "O.K.," she said, "now I know."

Then she went off on a Vision Quest for four nights and three days. The first day the skies became dark, and the air turned cold. It began to snow. The flurries thickened into a blizzard, cutting visibility to six feet.

Overwhelmed by the change, she nevertheless managed to set up her shelter and to get inside her sleeping bag, where she dozed through the oncoming night.

By morning the snow had abated somewhat, but everything was cloaked in white unfamiliarity. She could not make out her surroundings. She thought briefly about building a fire, but discovered she had thoughtlessly left half of her pack where the snow could get to it. Her matches were soaked. She was alone without heat for three days and nights in the wilderness of the headwaters of the Reese River, Nevada.

What did she do? She wept. She wept until the little valley echoed with the lost and lonely sound of her bird-like sobbing. I heard everything from my perch across the meadow where I had set up my shelter. Oh, it was cold. So cold that the sting of my fire could not dispel its embrace.

She wept intermittently for a day and a night. The next day she moved around a little. The weather improved. Snow turned to rain. Rain turned into partly cloudy spring skies. She managed finally to get her fire started, though it was mostly smoke.

Others had experienced difficulties, too. Ted, a young man from Novato, had fallen into the river upstream. Soaked to the bone, he walked several miles through the snow to get to the van, which he broke into, living there in misery for the remaining while.

Times were hard. We clung to our loneliness like bugs to an icy stone, insignificant, at the whim of the weather, which might squash us at any moment. Panic and loneliness rushed into our throats. But in the heart of the deepest pang, tiny lavender flowers pushed up through the snow and opened their petals to the freezing wind.

When the three days and nights were over, Liz came out, with five others who had persevered. She was not the same person. Her fingers were scarred and dirty. Her face was smeared with soot; stains of woodsmoke tears rimmed her eyes, which stared at me like two agates.

"How was it?" I asked.

She wiped the back of a black hand across her nose and a sly smile appeared. "All right," she said.

———————————

You Must Wait for Wisdom, Your Guide.

*Ask the blind worm the secrets of the
    grave, and
why her spires
Love to curl around the bones of death;
    and ask
the ravenous snake
Where she gets poison, and the winged
    eagle why he
loves the sun.
And then tell me the thoughts of man,
    that have
been hid of old.*
—William Blake, The Visions of the
    Daughters of Albion

The entire body of the Great Mother is clothed in symbols, rhythms and signs that are like solar collectors of human consciousness. The hero/ine of the Vision Quest moves among the motions of day and night, wind and silence, water and rock, air and fire, and seeks to gather wisdom from the things she/he has empowered with wisdom. If the hero/ine can but listen, the stones of the earth speak.

To obtain this wisdom, the past must be forgotten, the thought process must be stilled, clocks must stop. The hero/ine must enter the crack between the worlds, the universe that exists between illusion and reality. The hero/ine must be able to stop the internal dialogue in order to be receptive, for the treasure is not found by being distracted or fooled.

The attainment of wisdom, vision or insight is accomplished by persistence. The transformational teachings of Mother Nature are not won without a committed desire to learn and to apply what is learned. The hero/ine may wait and pray through the threshold with great resoluteness only to wring the smallest amount of comfort from the whirlwind. Yet the smallest insight may lead to the greatest victory after the hero/ine has recrossed the threshold and has reentered the mortal world to do battle with mortal dragons. More often than not, god spoke to the prophets of old in a "still, small voice." Such voices can be easily ignored or go unheard unless the hero/ine perseveres in the desire to hear. The story of Carey illustrates how wisdom patiently won during the Vision Quest was persistently applied to a successful end.

CAREY

Carey fell in love with a man who was twenty-eight. She was sixteen. Her parents knew nothing about it. She slept with him, loved him, and went to great lengths to be discreet. Meanwhile she attended high school and lived at home with her mother, with whom she felt some empathy, and her father, with whom she felt none.

An intelligent, attractive young woman, Carey tended to keep to herself, growing up just a little faster than her peers. Their incessant preoccupation with fashion and fast cars, their drunken parties and boasting exploits, were of little interest to her. "I'm not attracted to guys my age," she said. She was drawn to the mysterious world of an older man, learning aptly the lessons of a lover's attention.

But after a time the romance began to die. The older man turned out to be selfish and fatuous. He was threatened by her intensity, jealous of her world outside him. He was not able to set her free so that she could freely make a commitment to him. Stubbornly, she resisted his ways of dominating her, of trying to dictate her thinking as her father had done. Gradually she began to see that she had fallen into a cycle of dependence, hoping her lover would fill the void created by the abdication of her father.

She realized that she wanted to tell the older man that it was time to call it off, but she found herself unable to do so. He also had fallen into a cycle of dependence. He told her he loved her. She realized that a part of her loved him and cared about how he felt.

Caught up then in a dilemma which her young, fresh life magnified into despair, she heard about the Vision Quest. The idea of it began to take hold of her. She would be able to get away from it all, the anxieties of concealment, discretion, stolen love, the gnawing guilt, and live alone for three days and nights in some place where she could think clearly. She would have a chance to ponder the questions of who she was and where she was going, away from the measuring eyes of others.

She called to get information. She called again for more. She was persistent. She needed and wanted it. She could not wait. Two weeks before a Vision Quest was scheduled to leave for the desert, she was introduced to a group of strangers and took a crash course in first aid, fire making (she had never built one) and desert survival. The group, composed of students from another school, took her in, and she found a quiet place.

Shortly thereafter, she found herself in the Black Mountains of Death Valley, perched alone and exposed on a ledge beneath the ugly beautiful, tortured, steep, western face of Smith Mountain, with two gallons of water, a lumpy old down bag, several boxes of wooden strike-anywhere matches, a journal and a pen. She was not particularly well-prepared for this. She had never camped out anywhere before.

Of the three days and nights that followed, only she can tell. The weather was a little on the cold side. On the first day of the new year and the last day of her lonely vigil, the wind snarled and blew cold.

But we who waited at base camp saw and heard nothing of her. The days strolled by. The velvet-cold desert night illumined by a crescent moon came and went. We gazed into the twisted, alien massif of the Black Mountains and wondered, with an inner ache, how everybody was doing. The mountains answered our questioning with impassive menace. We exist, they said, whether you do or not.

Yet we knew that here and there, deposited in the folds and scales of the mountains, twelve tiny flames of human consciousness flickered.

Carey was out there. And on the morning of the fourth day she returned with her buddy, scratched and worn, but alive and well. As the others checked in, two-by-two, and the mountain silence was reclaimed by human laughter, the stories unfolded, intermingled, and burst into the windy sky.

Only Carey seemed quiet. There was an inwardness about her, a solemnness that indicated she had been through a struggle. Like others, her story was one of courage and frustration. Her shelter against the wind had not been adequate. Her sleeping bag, second-hand and lumpy, had not kept out the cold. No, she had not been able to get a fire going, despite her previous instruction. Yes, she had plenty of matches. But she went through the box of them, one by one. The wind blew them all out.

What did she do? Well, she looked at the mountains. She slept whenever she could. She thought a lot about her relationship with her lover. She went over and over it, worrying it down, as a dog does a bone. No, she had not seen any living thing but one small mouse. She had pulled her wool cap down over her ears, crouched on a ledge of Precambrian rock, and for three days and nights existed on the growing realization that she must leave her lover.

Several weeks after she came home, she got up the courage to show him the contents of the journal she had kept during her Vision Quest. It was all there: the perilous descent into self-affirmation, the fear of loss, the doubt, the pain, the loneliness, the self-examination. The desert was also there, in her words, paring down her meanings to the bare clarity of human self-preservation. Even as she had to leave her father, so she had to leave him.

Her lover read the journal, but he read with the eyes of a man who did not want to see. He read what he told himself were the words of a sixteen-year-old girl. "You're just being emotional about this," he said. He yawned, rolled over, and went to sleep.

But she persisted, gradually, fearfully, and in great pain. As she had gone through her box of matches, one by one, so she spent her resolve to be free of the man who might have taken the place of her father.

Within another month her lover had fallen in love with another woman. He transferred his attention to someone more comfortable, and Carey was finally free. But he kept her journal. He never gave it back.

In the following account, a young hero of the modern world crosses and recrosses the threshold, accumulating vitally needed power to effect changes within his life and the world around him. As Nature draws him into her secret heart, he begins to unfold himself and grow true.

LITTLE WARRIOR

Little Warrior was referred to us by Juvenile Probation. Actually, his referral was more like an ultimatum. In effect, the judge said, "Rites of Passage or Juvenile Hall."

Little Warrior, whose given name was Steve, was from a traditional Italian family. His grandfather was one of the moving forces behind banking interests in San Francisco. His father was personnel director of a large corporation. Both his mother and father cared what happened to him and were distressed that he had taken to drinking.

Steve was willing to talk freely and honestly about his personal problems. He described himself as a "pre-alcoholic." "If I take a drink I have to have another one. The trouble is, when I drink I do crazy things." Steve was well-known to the local police. He swore me to silence on a variety of capers that might have landed him in California Youth Authority. But he was not a "bad" boy.

There was something about Steve that made you like him no matter what he did. The father had the same gift, an irrepressible spirit, a knack for self-laughter. It was easy to want to root for Steve or go to bat when he was in trouble.

He had lots of problems with school. He did not like school, not even a little bit. He suffered from dyslexia, a learning disability. He fought his teachers tooth and nail and played the clown with his fellow students. The Vice Principal finally sent him to a Continuation School. That is when his probation officer called us up and brought him over.

We sat and talked about his going on a Vision Quest. You could see he was ready for something drastic. "Three days and nights alone, eh? Without eating?" He smiled slyly. "I'll kill a rabbit with a rock and sauté him in wild mushroom sauce." You could see he'd already figured it out. That is the way he was.

He came to all the pre-trip meetings, and when the big day arrived he showed up with his pack, a thirty pound inflatable rubber life raft, and a T-shirt with skull and crossbones across it and the legend: Black Death Lager.

Up, up, the trail wound, four miles to the spine of the South Warner Mountains. Steve, who had never backpacked before nor slept out under the stars, carried his load of seventy pounds without complaint. It was hard work, but he did it.

I was his buddy. The two of us shared a ridge above Emerson Lake. His place was in a nest of boulders looking out over the Surprise Valley. Our stonepile was on a slope covered with chalcedony and agate. The first day I went to check the stonepile, I found a note from him.

Good morning Steven
    I feel good. I am moving to the rocks for better shelter in case of rain. Last night I had fried grasshoppers. Not bad with garlic salt and oil. I leave with you on the rock pile my favorite throwing stones. I got a sunburn where the sun don't shine!

Take care
Little Warrior

P.S. I did hear coyotes

The second day I visited the rockpile, I found that he had left me another note.

good afternoon or morning
    I have a hard time sleeping. I keep thinking of my favorite pizza. I have stopped eating and I am joining the crowd. Tonite I am going to be on the ridge. Like my spot. Did you hear the sonic boom today? Scared the hell out of me. I was in the cave; it shook the whole joint.

Little Warrior
Little Fierce One

For a month after his Vision Quest Little Warrior did not drink at all. But then he began to drink and soon he was entangled with the law. His probation officer called again and two months later he was off with us, this time to the stark, sun-scoured canyons of Indian Pass in Death Valley. This trip he did not Vision Quest. He stayed in base camp and waited with me for the others to return. Most of the time he was alone, out on the desert pavement of the Amargosa, looking for arrowpoints and ancient stone alignments. Before the week was over he had found a large chert knife, several points (one of them Folsom-type), a sleeping circle (perhaps five thousand years old), a whole pocketful of obsidian and chert flakes, a chunk of lazulite, several fine examples of pre-1900 tin cans and a large piece of purple glass. He had participated three times in the tedious process of ferrying eight gallons of water from the bus to base camp, three miles away. When we returned, he gave the chert knife to me.

A month later he was back again, in the Black Mountains of Death Valley, where he vision quested for a second time, returning strong and proud. We began to hear comments like, "Steve has really changed." His behavior in school took a new turn. He organized the Madrone High School Mafia, a group that collected money for pizza, which was brought back and shared at lunch time with all.

He started showing up for things like benefit dinners, as part of the cooking crew. He dropped in one night to talk to a group of guys on probation who were contemplating a Vision Quest. "The Vision Quest isn't any trip for 'pussies,'" he told them. When we took a group of learning disabled people to the beach, he showed up and was overheard saying: "I've got a learning disability too—dyslexia. I have trouble going from left to right."

I have lost count of the number of trips Little Warrior has taken. All I know is I like this young man. I would trust him with my baby daughter. I've stopped asking him about his drinking. Somehow the question does not fit the man he has become.

Last month we took a group, including Little Warrior, to Indian Pass. It was not a Vision Quest group; it was a group of adults from the local community college. We were following an ancient Indian route through the Funeral Mountains, migrating from east to west. Finding the road into the mouth of the pass had been washed out, we stopped the bus ten miles short and unloaded our packs.

The plan was for me to let everybody else off and then to drive the bus back down into Death Valley, around the Funerals and south to a point where the group, descending through the pass, would come upon it at the end of the trek. I would leave the bus there and hike the opposite way, up through the pass, and rejoin the group camped at the eastern mouth.

But we had a problem. The washout had caused us to stop short of our goal. The hike to the mouth of the pass would be much longer. From our position it was impossible to see the destination, a low point on the horizon

127

amid a jumble of crags and peaks. Two of us had a sense of how to get there, having been there before: Little Warrior and me. But I had to drive the bus back. That left Little Warrior.

He and I climbed to the top of the bus and looked westward to the swell of the horizon, trying to pinpoint the location of the pass. A couple of hills, six or seven miles out to the right, seemed vaguely familiar. We agreed it would be best to walk in a westerly direction keeping to the left of these hills. When darkness came, the group would have to stop and camp. He and Meredith would be the leaders of the group. He would take over my place while I was away. Meredith, who was unfamiliar with the area, would back up Steve's decisions regarding the proper way to proceed.

I left them then, backing the bus away from the brink of the washout, and pointed my nose away from the little band of modern immigrants moving toward a small canyon entrance among a maze of canyons lost in the immensity of the Amargosa Desert. As I left, a rain squall hit.

Several hours later, as the sun was going down, I left the bus west of the canyon mouth along the main road to Furnace Creek. With a pack and two gallons of water I headed toward the western mouth of the pass, four miles away. By the time it was completely dark, I was at the western entrance to Indian Pass. Sleeping there for the night, I continued in the morning, pacing myself with hard, fast hiking rhythms, testing my body. The canyon narrowed, became steeper. As I ascended I kept hearing voices in the cool, gloomy recesses of the canyon.

I was driven ahead by a kind of anxiety, fearing that somehow all was not well with the party out on the desert coming toward the pass. By mid-afternoon I had reached Poison Spring and began to seek a way to ascend a ridge, to get high, to look out across the vast bowl of the Amargosa to see if I could spy the party. Finding a ridge, I climbed it, with the help of a bighorn sheep trail along the upper slopes. When I reached the top, the sun was low in the west. The Amargosa lay before me to the east, bright and warm in the rays of the setting sun. I looked for a long time, but saw no one.

Then I heard a shout. I was unable to ascertain its direction, but the hearing of it spurred me on. Two hours later at sundown, I found the group camped exactly where Steve said he would bring them. Facing disagreement from other members in a group that included two medical doctors and the quality control director of a large corporation, he had insisted that he knew the way. As it turned out, he did.

———————

Then Your Eyes Will Be Opened. You Will See What You Have to Give, What You Must Do.

He whose face gives no light, shall never become
a star.
—*William Blake,* Proverbs of Hell

The gift to give, the trail to follow, is revealed to the hero/ine when the eyes are opened and the quester sees with the eyes of eternity. The name of the gift is no secret: the gift of love. But it is one thing to know about love; it is another to see with the eyes of eternity. The modern hero/ine, living in a mythically impoverished culture, is nevertheless capable of experiencing mystical insight, of seeing with opened eyes what it is that binds the self and all things together in oneness.

The following account clearly indicates the mythical potential of the Vision Quest. Not everyone, however, is necessarily gifted with the ability to experience mystical insight. For reasons known only by the Great Mother, this young heroine was given one of life's greatest prizes.

GLOWING MOUNTAIN IN THE DAWN

DECEMBER 31.
I find myself constantly thinking about friends and family, but I feel good about not being with them right now. I miss mom. I really want her to be here so she can see how beautiful this desert is. I've learned so much about colors and shadows and shapes from her. The mountain range across from me is silhouetted by the last glint

of light from the sun. There is just a sliver of a moon suspended above it. A faint twinkle from a few stars and violet-hued clouds decorate the sky. Mom, it's really here; it's gorgeous. I give it to you in spirit, and a lot of love along with it.

I miss you, dad. I think a lot about how you would take to fasting. I don't know how I will either. I'm so glad you introduced the kids to Mother Nature at such an early age.

I feel that . . . part of my whole family is with me on this quest. Each member makes up a little of who I am.

JANUARY 1.
Last night. Well, I say now that I was horribly afraid. Of what? After I got in my bag and snuggled in tight, I heard footsteps. I could have sworn someone was coming toward my camp. I stuck my head out, not even breathing for fear he'd hear me. Nothing. Nobody. Stuck my head back in. Then I came to the conclusion that these "footsteps" were the pace of my heart. I remember mom telling me once that I should think of the rhythms of my heart as something peaceful. I'm alive!

I feel wonderfully at peace—with myself, with Nature. Today as I was exploring I kept talking to the mountains. They are so majestic and seem to know life. I asked them questions. A deafening silence was their answer. They couldn't tell me what to do, but they let me decide for myself. . . .

As I was coming back up the mountain, I began to gather wood for the evening. All of a sudden a huge, gusty wind came up from the north. I made it as far as the peak below the one I'm on, and then had to throw the wood down and huddle against part of the cliff. The mountain underneath me began to shake. I began to shake. That wind was powerful. I really could have lost my balance and died trying to scale that cliff in the gust.

JANUARY 2.
Night came on. I built no fire. I placed my rocks into a circle starting at north, then south, to east, then west. Each time I set a rock in its place, I gave my cry: "Dear Father, We need!"

I let my mind drift, with no preconceptions of what I would see. Little happy memories came to me. It seemed that my child-

131

hood was suddenly unfolded before me. I saw my growth through the sadness and joy experienced in that past. I felt at peace, content with the spirit I had become. I no longer felt that parts of my past should have been different. Then came the little images. I got so tired that I dozed off: two, fifteen, thirty minutes at a time.

In one image, I saw a candle burning. It slowly transformed itself into an old-fashioned kerosene lamp, then into a light bulb. History, eternal ideas, the promise of the progress of Love—I felt them all.

I saw a bright, fiery ball. There was a black hole in the middle of it. I felt my whole being rushing, as if vacuumed, toward that hole. I entered it. Blackness all around me. So peaceful. The feeling of being received, accepted. I opened my eyes. I was *here,* on Earth! I realized that that image symbolized my Passage. I was born to this exciting, beautiful, ugly, dangerous, receiving Earth.

But why have I denied this feeling of becoming one with the world? I have been so afraid of feeling naked, stripped of my status, my security from home, my pride, my old confidence, my feeling I controlled the world around me.... Those things were my supposedly indestructible foundation. But as I am learning from the mountains, eventually what seems to look like a secure, sturdy rock will crumble under too much force. Someday it will succumb.

I looked at the moon—a glowing crescent. I actually saw a pure, shining dove rise out of it and descend to Earth! I had my eyes wide open. I saw that beautiful bird flying down toward the planet. I closed my eyes and screamed: "Dear Father, We need!" I thought that the image was a hallucination. I was afraid to believe in such a powerful sight.

Then it clicked. I was sitting there in my bag in the blackness. My head was tilted up toward the sky and stars, and my eyes were closed. I began to feel raindrops on my closed eyelids. Then, still with my eyes shut, I saw triangular, no, pyramid-shaped figures of light traveling from every direction, heading for my eyes, going through my eyes into my soul. I felt a surge of power, of awareness.

I opened my eyes. Those brilliant stars were still sending down pyramids of energy to me—I saw it all clearly. Like a river, there was a constant flow of that warmth, power and light coming directly from the stars into my being, through my eyes.

Everything just seemed to click. The Spirit (I call it God) sent me that mystical message: Love. He gave me that reason why I'm here on earth. This wonderful planet gives us the place to not only exist as a life form, but to grow together. I'm here to participate in that potential fellowship. I'm here to Love and accept. Through those images — the stars, the sun, all this energy in the world — I can collect it within me, and direct it to humanity.

The hero/ine enters the threshold incomplete. Via the solitary heroic journey through the body of the Great Mother, the seeker is healed, made complete. The gift cannot be given to others until the self is whole and well. Love cannot be imparted until the self is loved.

Sometimes the dragon to be encountered is lack of self-love, that is, self-destructiveness. Ultimate victory over certain kinds of self-destructive behavior, particularly those which are addicting, is not won in a single fracas. The dragon appears and reappears to claim its victims, and the only way to fight it is with the rage of love and self-respect. Words and high intentions are not sufficient.

The hero/ine engages the dragon of self-destruction in a battle. By learning how to win, the seeker learns how to fight. Learning how to fight, the seeker learns how to live. Learning how to live, the seeker learns how to die.

Graham, the hero of the following story, is living today in Marin County. He engaged the dragon of self-destruction during a Vision Quest to Nevada several years ago. He may never be entirely free of his dragon; but he crossed the threshold and was given the gift of wellness, of completeness. He saw what he had to do. Then, fearful as any hero, knowing all too well the gigantic proportions of his own personal dragon, he stepped back across the threshold to do battle.

GRAHAM

He was a nice guy — and he was a heroin addict. He was in a therapeutic community of ex-junkies when he first heard about the Vision Quest. From the beginning he was the most enthusiastic about stretching his muscles and living

133

alone with the forces of Nature. All his counselors said it would do him good.

Socially he was a star, a vital, magnetic man who spoke candidly and with intelligence. But nobody knew what he would do when he left the support system and friends of the therapeutic community and went back alone to the streets of San Rafael, where his old junkie friends were still lurking for a fix, anxious to prove he was no better than they.

So he went to the headwaters of the Reese River in Nevada's Toiyabe Mountains with a bunch of other friends from the therapeutic community, with his counselor, Al, and a nurse, Angela (to dispense methadone to those who required it). While he was there he took to the mountains like a snake to a warm rock. He caught his limit of Rainbows and Eastern Brooks with worms he scavenged from the banks of Upper Sawmill Creek. He slept in the hollow of a willow tree. He hiked up the ravines and came back with arrow-points in his hands. He ate like a horse and slept like a lamb. "This is the life for me," he declared, and talked about becoming a cowboy. If he was a star in his therapeutic community, he was a blossom in the high desert.

When he came back from his Vision Quest, he seemed bigger than life. It had been a good time for him, a time of self-testing and self-analysis. The late summer sun was strong and pure. It burned the impurities from his body. The fasting cleansed him from within. He had picked wild rosehips from the bushes growing near the river and made strong, sweet tea. His eyes were clear and alert, like an animal's; his body was lean and brown. He looked damn good.

That night, after the giving away and the numerous stories, he announced that he was not going back. The city held no more interest for him. He would stay here, maybe hire on at one of the ranches down in the valley.

We talked about going back then, for a long time, as the fire exhaled sweet juniper and the stars danced their slow ballet across the sands of forgetful night. The real monster, we decided, was fear of going back to face the monster.

The next morning we hiked out. It was a sad time. As we ascended the canyonside, the river glistened like a green snake shedding a skin of willows. "I'll always remember what I learned here," vowed Graham.

A month later he graduated from the therapeutic community and went to live in San Rafael, working up in Petaluma cleaning out chicken coops. He rode the bus to and from work, came home exhausted every night. He took up with his old girl friend, the same one who had first introduced him to heroin. He told us he was staying clean.

I went over to his place a couple of times. It was a depressing apartment with no windows and a TV set at one end. At the other end was a shrine: a little picture-altar with a deer skull, a pair of antlers, obsidian flakes, and photos and mementos of his Vision Quest. He talked vaguely about getting out to Pt. Reyes or up to Yosemite, but he seemed full of inertia and sodden with self-disgust at the grind he found himself in. He smoked a lot.

A couple of months later, I read about him in the newspaper. He and his old lady had been caught with stolen goods and an "undisclosed quantity of heroin." He was back in jail, back where he had started.

For a long time I heard nothing of him. Then three years later he passed me on the freeway. He was driving an old but respectable pickup truck with a tool box in the back. "Hey," he yelled excitedly. "Hey!" I yelled back at him, "how're you doing?"

He hung his head out the window with a big grin on his face and hollered, "I'm clean!"

You Must Return to Your People and Give Away to Them.

Eternity is in love with the production of time.
—*William Blake*, Proverbs of Hell

The return from the threshold is no less heroic than the act of severance. The hero/ine must return to the same mother world, but no longer attached to it in the same way. The problem becomes the maintaining of the visionary standpoint in the face of immediate earthly pain or joy. The taste of the fruits of the temporal draws the attention away from the threshold and fixes it on the peripheral crisis of the moment. The balance of perfection is lost. To complete the heroic journey, the returning hero/ine must survive the impact of the world.

There is a gift to give away, a vision to perform, a path to follow, a dragon to slay, a light to bear. The reincorporation of the hero/ine requires that she/he demonstrate the power and effectiveness of the vision:

> I think I have told you, but if I have not, you must have understood, that a man who has a vision is not able to use the power of it until after he has performed the vision on earth for the people to see.
> —Black Elk

At the return threshold the transcendental power must be left behind. The

136

gift that is given is the self, an active, mortal force applied among human beings of flesh and blood. The miraculous is manifested, not by divine intervention, but by taking one human step at a time. If the hero/ine must return to a world of death, then the gift given is love, love that transcends death.

SILENCE

On the top of South Caribou Mountain there is a small clearing of sand. A crooked tree with a low branch becomes a shelter from wind and unexpected rain. Red ants live in a large lava rock.

From 7,761 feet, according to the USGS map of 1934, you can see a hundred miles in every direction, including Mt. Shasta, Mt. Lassen and the far lights of civilization in the southwestern distance. In the morning, first to see the sun. At the end of the day, last to breathe in darkness.

I stayed three days alone, fasting on the peak, spending my time writing in my journal, meditating, walking down the ridge to make sculptures at the rock pile, praying for living things, including the earth, and just sitting around thinking and looking into my heart and out at the world.

The first evening I built a fire even before the sun had set. I wrote then, "The fire is a blessing. The smoke reminds me of our campfires earlier in the week and of good people." I went to sleep early, knowing my shelter was a good shield from the wind which would rush over the mountain. Whether it would do much good if it rained, I didn't know. That night it did rain for an hour or so, and by scrunching my body under the very low branch I stayed dry and slept well considering my somewhat contorted position.

I had a dream that night. . . . I saw an old friend and he called me into his office, and I told him I had to hurry to be at work at St. Vincent's (a residential treatment center for emotionally disturbed boys). He read me a letter in the Examiner from someone named Gustave Cesoni. There was a guy named John Cesoni when we went to school in Illinois. Seems Gustave or John had asked for my help. He had been injured somehow. A car accident? He was hurt either near Indian Valley (Novato, CA) or Santa Barbara. I think I said it wasn't that close to me and I had to go to work.

Coming back to civilization I was naturally high, happy and filled with a sense of power and strength. I walked into my parent's house, eyes wide, a week's growth of beard bristling, telling tales of fire and mountain.

The next day I had to go back to work at St. Vincent's School. After a week in the woods, I was not particularly looking forward to working once again and voiced this feeling to my mother and brother. My mother looked at me and said, "I'm afraid there's some bad news at St. Vincent's. One of the kids died at camp."

"One of *my* kids?" I asked, as I began to pace around the house, my mind a whirl, my body moving, not wanting to fully hear the news nor hear which kid was gone. In my mind I began to picture each kid, thinking about my life and their lives and my quest for a vision, going around the house, going crazy, trying to collect myself.

"Who?" I asked the inevitable question.

"Sinetti."

I didn't know what to do. Sinetti. Sinetti Melson. He had drowned in the swimming pool. Sinetti, a beautiful, troubled, ten-year-old black kid, wiry, muscular, smiling, hating, wanting to be a major league baseball player, and with his cannon arm, great speed and bat, he actually could have been, if he could have controlled his anger, if he had only lived long enough. Sinetti was the best athlete (and dancer) in the house. How could a kid who could turn one and a halfs off the diving board with ease drown in a swimming pool?

At this point I felt I had two choices. I could either go crazy, meaning everything I believed in, the Vision Quest, myself, etc., would now be false, or else I could stay strong and deal with this. I knew I had to walk up the hill behind my house, which I had named Lew Welch Mountain. I had spent a lot of time on the hill, praying, singing, talking to the earth and sky, but I had never spent a night up there. Now I knew that I must do so. I couldn't return to civilization quite yet. . . .

138

My mind reeled on the top of Lew Welch Mountain. . . . I talked to Sinetti, recalling good times (playing catch, going to his baseball game, bringing him up to the house so he could get all duded up to dance in front of the whole school) and hard times like the last night I worked before the trip, when Sinetti and another boy were causing trouble after bedtime. I put him in bed. He jumped up and picked up a chair, losing his temper, starting on one of his rages. Finally he did settle down, and the next day we could be friends again.

I began to discover power on that hill. Sinetti was dead. I was making peace with him, expressing my sorrow his life was so short. I knew I would not go crazy, and that here was my vision—death—and that I must draw strength from Sinetti's life and death.

In the morning I walked down the hill and went to St. Vincent's where I met two other counselors and waited for the kids to return from summer camp. We would have to deal with our own emotions and those of the kids. Many of the kids had an idea he was gone already. When we told them, one blurted out, "Hooray," not understanding what he was saying. Others cried, including his roommate. We tried to find out as much information as possible about what happened, who saw what, trying to make sure no one felt responsible for the death. Quiet talk lasted into the evening. We looked at a few pictures of Sinetti. One close friend said, "I've never had a best friend die before." It was a trying day of return into this world.

Looking back on my dream of "Cesoni" getting hurt, it struck me clearly that on some level I was in touch with what was happening or would happen to one of my people. There is death in this world, and it must touch near me often and one day touch me directly.

I will draw strength from those people I come in contact with; even when they are gone their spirit is with me.

I will draw strength from the places of my Vision Quest, even when I am far away.

I will work, pray, and sing for my people.

I will love, let go, and continue loving.

I will work, pray, and sing that my people, and the earth, may
fully live.

Who can say what lies ahead when the threshold is recrossed? Further ahead
(who can say how far?) lurks the ultimate dragon of the hero/ine's death.
She/he returns as she/he went out, courageously entering, mastering the art
of walking in balance between what was and what will be, preparing to face
what surely will be, death and the ultimate transformation.

PETE

He must have weighed 300 pounds. He was overweight, Jewish, and from
Long Island, New York. He had moved to the West Coast recently with his
mother and brothers and did not get along well at the regular high school. He
cut classes, smoked dope, and bummed around the streets of San Rafael, his
hands in his pockets. Rarely did he spend time at home. His mother, who
worked late at night, saw him occasionally on the weekends.

What he did on his lonely jaunts is anybody's guess. He never got in
trouble with the police. But he did get in trouble with the school authorities,
who were forced to deal with his prolonged absences. Bound by law, the
authorities sent him to a "Continuation School."

It was at Continuation School that we met him. We had gone there to
introduce the idea of a Vision Quest course. A group gradually formed,
including Pete.

You could see he was struggling to keep his feet among his peers. They
laughed at him behind his back and made snide, cutting jokes about his
weight. But somehow he was holding on, tenaciously, having finally found,
among a school of rummies, burn outs, hustlers, low riders, and dissatisfied,
disillusioned, frightened, intelligent students, a place to learn.

He turned out to be a bright young man, gifted with the ability to
adapt, to assert himself, to make his way, to make friends, to be a fixture. He

rolled with the punches. He was always ready with a story to match the one you told. Somehow you doubted his veracity, but not his sincerity. He was a good person, with a warm heart, who gave gifts and made contacts. He became Vice President In Charge of Making Sure Everybody Knew What Was Going On. He began to drop by the house regularly, uninvited, only to fall asleep in the rocking chair in front of the fire.

When the time came he declared himself ready and went into the Inyo Mountains with two other buddies, seeking the upper reaches of a canyon, where he would separate and live alone for two days and nights. Nobody's expectations were particularly high. It was a difficult canyon they had chosen, and neither Pete nor his buddies, Scott and Dave, were in the best of shape. We said goodbye to them and took off, leaving them to look up at the eastern flank of the Inyos.

A day later we heard the news, via a note left along the roadway in a bottle, that they had spent the night elsewhere and were anxious to get back to civilization. It was alleged that Pete had encountered a wild-eyed spectre in an old cabin they stumbled across. "It's not time yet!" the spectre reportedly screamed at him. We decided to let them alone, to see what would happen, and heard nothing more from them until the two days and nights were up.

Their stories were tall and their faces were brown. Pete looked great. He was twenty pounds lighter and his pants were ripped up the crotch. They had decided to go up the canyon after all, where, stopped by "immense, impassable walls," they camped. Apparently, they spent the last day and night apart, for Pete spoke glowingly of his "Vision Quest," which he might have embroidered a bit with stories of face to face meetings with a bobcat, an eagle, several tarantulas, a rattlesnake seven feet long, and a wicked clump of devil's head cactus.

Two weeks later we got a call. It was Pete. Yes, everything was O.K. at home. He and Mike would be up for a visit in a couple of hours. We were working and not much interested in seeing anyone, so we hardly missed them when they did not show. A day later we found out why they did not.

Thumbing a ride north to our house on Highway 101, they were picked up by a man in a late model pickup truck. Pete seemed to know him, but once they were well away it became evident that the man was dangerously drunk. The drunk accelerated his truck to ninety miles an hour and began weaving uncontrollably.

They pleaded with him to pull over and let them out, but he was too far gone. Braking, swerving to avoid a rear end collision, he lost control and the truck hurtled end over end, like a tin can kicked across the highway.

Miraculously, Mike was unhurt; the driver was critically injured; Pete was instantly killed.

BOOK 5

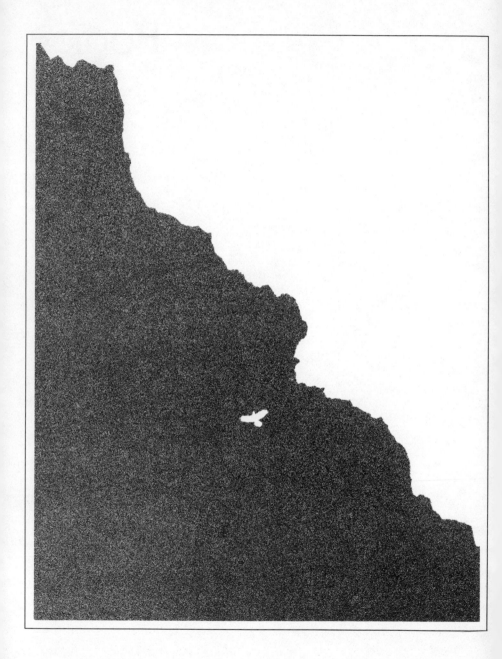

5. THE VISION

When you have discovered the mountain, the first
miracle that will appear is this. A most vehement
and very great wind, that will shake the mountain
and shatter the rocks to pieces. You shall be
encountered also by lions and dragons and other
terrible beasts, but fear not any of these things. Be
resolute and take heed that you return not, for . . .
after all these things and near the daybreak there
shall be a great calm, and you shall see the Day-Star
arise and the dawning will appear, and you shall
perceive a great treasure. The chiefest thing in it,
and the most perfect, is a certain exalted tincture,
with which the world . . . might be tinged and
turned into most pure gold.
—Eugenius Philalethes, Lumen de Lumine, 1651

The time had come. He knew it. Deep down in the quick, he knew he *had* to go. All the signs were there: loss of purpose, desperation arising from an inability to live up to his own ideals, lack of faith, numbness, vague and sourceless anxiety, thoughts of suicide, disappointment in love, a sense of failure, not only in the world's eyes, but in his own. Was it that his life lacked risk? He was disturbed by the thought. But how could he risk anything amid the responsibilities he had assumed?

This man had enjoyed worldly success. He had lived off the fat of the land, unthinking as a tick. Striving for prizes, he had succeeded in a way, only to find boredom and self-mockery. His sleep was disturbed by dreams of people he had never seen and places he had never been. His waking days were spent hoping for some unattainable fulfillment just around the corner.

Then he began to break away, to think about risking his life. What was the goal? To be someone more than who he was. To be someone more in his own eyes.

So he surrendered his work, settled his accounts with others, set his house in order, said farewell to his wife, children and friends. He put a few necessary things in a knapsack and prepared to leave the town he lived in, to leave his life of tomorrows and yesterdays and go off into the wilderness, the land of todays, to seek a vision.

The trail began at the front door of his home, through which he walked. His loved ones held him in an embrace that was loving and dangerous. He loved them but he could not remain there. He had already begun to climb the mountain. There was no turning back.

Pathetically his children called to him, "Have mercy on us. We are starving and have nothing to eat." He cursed himself and kept walking. He had nothing to feed them.

His wife turned in her sleep and felt for his familiar body. He was not there. She awoke and called his name. He heard her, but he would not reverse his course.

The mountain he wanted to climb is called the Mountain of the Heart. It was steep and discouraging, yet beautiful and inviting. It was near at hand, yet far away. He set a course for a far-off ridge and cried for the memory of home.

Presently he came to a dark cave framed by a jumble of rocks and boulders. He entered the cave, and the darkness of the place took away his eyes and gave him blindness by which to see. In the midst of the confusion of his blindness, the image of his mother appeared to him, radiant, dressed in her wedding dress. She seemed forever beautiful and forever young.

"Here is your heart," she said. "I gave it to you when you were born. You must have it for your journey. Without it you cannot complete your quest. It is a seed," she said, "to be planted in the earth of your body." She held the heart out to him and beckoned him to take it. "This is your spiritual food," she said.

He realized suddenly that he was to eat his heart. The idea was not greatly abhorrent to him. The heart was of his own substance and yet seemed insubstantial. He took the glowing, living thing in his hand and crushed it to his mouth. He swallowed. He swallowed again. He could not swallow it down. Suddenly he felt choked and hysterical. He could not swallow his heart. It was caught in his throat.

He clutched at this throat, as if to squeeze his heart from it. He called for his mother, but her image had faded into the blindness.

Against the velvet walls of unseeing he began to weep. And as he wept he felt a keen sensation at the core of his throat, a feeling of pain and joy, as though his throat were welling up with the tears of humankind.

When he finally reappeared at the mouth of the cave, light was falling into the darkness of the west. The evening star tolled in a deep blue sky. Now, more than ever in his life, he felt alone. His mother was gone. An old life was fading into the curtain of memory. Come what may, he was alone.

In his loneliness, he tried to call out a prayer to the west, the prayer his children had taught him: "Have mercy on me. I am starving and have nothing to eat." But he could not utter the words; his heart was stuck in his throat. The mountain he had to climb was stuck in his throat.

He sank to his knees in dismay. The cool dusk and its first smattering of stars offered scant consolation. He looked up into the shadowy bulk of the mountain that was stuck in his throat. How could he ever climb that mountain?

He was able to see his life with greater clarity then: the women he had loved, the friendships he had forged or forsaken, the dashed hopes, the thwarted ambitions, the self-pity. His life heaved in on him, a dark heavy burden of karma. The mountain looming up defied his skill and challenged his little faith. "You are but a scrap of meat to be pecked to pieces by the raven of Death," said the mountain to him. "How have you made yourself worthy to climb me?"

The moon arose, a horned owl perched on a bough of darkness. He looked up at the mountain and sighed. He could not, would not, separate himself from his quest. The wind blew fresh and a little cool. He resumed his climb, as the twilight deepened.

He had not gone far before he came across a rattlesnake. The rattle-snake, who was hunting, had noticed him long before, as a rumble in the earth and an approaching warmth in the air. The snake had curled into a defensive posture, warning the intruder.

It was a Panamint rattler, salmon and dun, a male in his prime. He had been born live and sleek from his mother, who had chosen not to linger with her litter, but had left them to fend for themselves. His enemies were many; his friends were few. Fated to travel without leg, foot, or claw, he had survived by depending on instinct, unable, when on the hunt, to protect himself from the sudden claws from the air that would rivet him to the rock with thorns of steel.

Gifted with an uncanny ability to stalk, paralyze, kill, swallow and digest, he was also motivated by his soul to shake the rattle fixed to his tail whenever danger lurked on the wind. This self-defeating gesture, this warning to others, even a creature of such infinitely dangerous capabilities as a human being, was both foolhardy and graceful, an unjustifiable act of mercy: the lesser knight bravely standing his ground and waiting in the open, nobly refusing to lurk, or to strike from the back.

The two stared at each other in the night. Neither wanted to harm the other. Each hoped merely to pass by. Impassively noble, the snake rattled louder. "Pass by!"

I have no intention to harm you, thought the man. I am compelled to climb this mountain. Your presence in my path leads me to believe you are here to teach me. I seek to transform myself, to be more than I am, to be new.

"I have shed many skins," said the snake. "I hope to shed many more. I live upon the sand, hiding in the rock, waiting like silence for the appearance of life with which to fill my hunger."

Death will reward your search, the man thought bitterly. Death will stoop on you with a pair of feathered claws. Death will satisfy your hunger, even as it will satisfy mine. You, snake, will die with grace and abandon. What about me?

The snake shifted and drew himself into a tighter circle of power and tested the palpable air. "I shall be neither quick to strike nor slow," he warned. "I shall not hesitate. I am not at war within myself, divided between body and mind. I am what I do, and I do it well."

Sensing a new menace in the snake, the man drew away, though he was by far the stronger, and went on. The waning moon spread a path and the stars pressed him close.

He trudged ahead, the only sounds his panting breath and scrambling footfalls. Above him the mountain was etched in dull silver. The going was not easy. He became hot and sweaty beneath his clothing. The dark wind cooled, then chilled him. He found a small gully and a juniper growing from a projecting ledge, the boughs of the tree spreading down to form shelter. From his knapsack he took a blanket and lay down in the soft, fragrant bed of needles. As he sank into sleep he observed that the stars were becoming obscured by clouds.

He did not awaken to the glow of morning light. He awoke to the flash of a bolt of lightning. He sat upright, ears ringing with the sound of thunder.

A late spring storm was drifting in from the west. The moon and the stars were gone. From dark, massed clouds came a scatter of rain and wind, then down, down around his ears the storm came, sweeping the ridges with its broom of lightning, tearing loose boulders of thunder from the cliffs of the sky.

Alone in his wretched little place the man began to weep from fear and helplessness. Nowhere could he hide. From childhood he had retained a terror of lightning and now he was forced to watch, like a cornered animal, the delicate, probing fingers of death.

The landscape flickered in stark negative. His tree appeared to be the only one for miles, his ledge the most exposed. His scalp began to tingle and his hair to rise. Too easily he imagined his body to be a lightning rod. He tried to pray.

The terror he felt was beyond telling. In the end he had to let go, to surrender to forces incomprehensible to him. The storm raged on, blinding the darkness with livid light. He was but an insect, a mosquito to be smashed against the stone. Faced by the realization of the meager conditions of his existence, he finally could not hold on to his life. When he was ready to die, the storm subsided, the mist fell away. Morning light flooded the east. He was alive, not by intention but by miracle. Aloft on the blue winds a raven greeted the new day.

But something in the man had changed. The storm had shocked him into an extended and heightened awareness of the magnitude of his love for life, which he now felt as extreme exhaustion. It had been an ordeal. He had seen the eyes of death, a blinding white. He had shriveled from fear of those bottomless eyes. He had experienced the frailty of life and surrendered to the element of death.

The morning sun seized him with drowsiness. The animal in him felt a torpid desire to curl up on a warm rock and sleep. He drowsed and slept like any wretch lucky to be alive, sprawled without thought on the verge of nothingness.

When he awoke the sun was high in the sky. He was uncomfortably warm. He took a sip of tepid water from his flask and realized the level was low. He would have to find water.

Directing his gaze along a ridge he saw where rains had cut deep into the flesh of the mother mountain. One canyon appeared dry. The other canyon, though steeper, held more promise. Up the ravine, up a dry wash streaking down from some old wound in the mountain, he could see a patch of bright green.

The way down the ridge and up the canyon, however, proved to be difficult and required great effort. As he had eaten nothing, the man was weak and dizzy. By the time he reached the green area, he was dusty and played out.

He arrived at a mesquite tree and a large growth of willows and reeds, certain signs of the presence of water. The air smelled damp. He got down on his knees among the willow shoots and dug his fingers through the lush inter-twining of reeds and shadows, but he was unable to discover more than a small mud hole.

Knowing he must have water or die, he began to scoop out the mud from the hole. Gradually, water began to rise within the depression until the hole was filled with dusky liquid, which, when allowed to settle, turned clear.

He looked long into the tiny pool and saw, at the bottom, flecks of chert magnified in the waterlight, glittering amid the roots and stems of the vegetation. The little bank upon which he leaned was soft and hidden, the color of coolness. Tiny purple flowers no bigger than freckles pushed up from the moss.

He lay down on his belly, in the crush of tall reeds and willows, and drank the water. It was profoundly satisfying water, hinting of mineral from the dark earth. He drank as long as he wished.

When his thirst was quenched and his flask full, the grateful man rested beneath the shade of the mesquite tree and contemplated his world. He looked at his dusty clothes. Dirty and wretched, he felt almost happy. Early afternoon breezes crept up under his shirt and hair. A hummingbird droned in the tops of the mesquite, where long, greenish flowers were blossoming into fruit.

Born of a venerable mother and the earth, germinated by the greedy feet of bees, the soul of the mesquite tree had fallen to the earth in the form of a honey bean. Slowly the bean had deteriorated, eaten away by tiny worms and raindrops, finally releasing its hoard of iron-like seeds. Winter came, and then early spring, with occasional thundershowers scattering the seeds and washing them down the canyon, away from the precious, life-sustaining moisture of the spring.

But one seed escaped the diaspora. One tough little soul unto itself held an obscure purchase, its purpose known only to the Heart of the Universe. And oblivious to all but survival, that hungry, determined little soul held on through a mean, wet winter, and gradually began to gnaw on the soil.

The seed, true to its nature, began to climb the mountain. With the coming of spring it quickened from within, stirred by the presence of another mountain without, a mountain of pure light. Before it had done climbing, it had traveled as far down into the earth as up to the sky. While ascending its graceful, branching ladder of light, it was giving birth to children: long, twisting honey beans. These sunburned beans ripened in the hardwood boughs and hung in the heat of the day and the cool of the night. Wild ambrosia, they beckoned the deer and bighorn sheep and the ghosts of Indians.

Yearning to fulfill herself, the mesquite fulfilled others, among them the human fruit of America, the peoples with names like Paiute, Mohave, Yuma, Cocopa, Pima, Papago and Seri. In their hands her fruit became meal, gruel, broth, pudding, bread, drink and joy juice. She was boiled and washed in sore eyes and open wounds. She was smoothed on chapped lips, cracked fingers, open blisters and sunburn. Her fruit was ground down into a fine powder and applied to the navels of newborn children. For this and so much more she was revered and worshiped. How many could not have lived without her!

And so gracefully and guilelessly did she assume her purpose, that the man who reclined beneath her did not give one thought to the truth that grew above and beneath him. But something of her soul, something beneath ordinary awareness passed into him – perhaps it was nothing more than her dappled coolness, the whisper of early afternoon wind in her leaves, her staunch yielding to the sun. He partook of her and felt, intermingled with his compulsive yearning, a sense of calm and unjustified, unmerited favor.

It was deeply pleasant to lie in the shade and indulge his exerted body. It seemed he had been climbing the mountain for years. The blue sky soothed him with a vast indifference. How unimportant in the scheme of things he was, tucked away in a tiny, forgotten pocket of the mountain.

Glancing idly around, he saw that his foot had dislodged a stone, beneath which an earthworm lay in the moist indenture, half-concealed. He plucked the worm from the soil and held its small coolness in the palm of his hand.

"Lowly earthworm," he addressed the creature, "I am no more important in the scheme of things than you." He said this in mock drama, not realizing that the common creature he thus addressed was, in fact, a being of great consequence. And though the worm neither saw nor heard him, it certainly sensed him – with an ancient wisdom of its kind that no human could ever fathom.

For this worm was hundreds of millions of years old, with an innate method of survival instilled in its nervous system long before there were humans on earth. This common earthworm was a near-perfect evolutionary adaption: the *Annelida* ("rings"), who stands out through history as the single creature most responsible for the survival of all living things. A master alchemist, the earthworm performs the magical function by which death and decay are transformed into fertile earth, the sacred womb of seeds. This it does by eating, digesting, and excreting its food in the form of castings. These castings have buried the earth many times over in richness.

A body of interconnected rings, or *somites,* makes the earthworm a veritable pile driver, able to move obstacles up to sixty times its own weight. A denizen of the underground, the worm has blue, photosensitive cells in its

152

head to bend its course always away from the sunlight and down into cool, moist, dark, ravenous byways, where, starving and with nothing to eat, it performs its ceaseless, sacred, magical quest.

Of course the man did not know or think of this, or he would not have absent-mindedly tossed the earthworm beyond the lifesaving shade of the mesquite. There, in the full sunlight, it died within sixty seconds.

It might have died forgotten. But the man, deciding finally to resume his quest, spied the lifeless form of the creature on a rock. He saw that it was dead and realized that he had killed it.

He picked it up again. The corpse had begun to smell. He had murdered the worm while it was on quest. It had begun to form a cocoon around the clitellum (sex organ). In a short while it would have given birth to twin young. Of this the man was also largely ignorant. He knew only a moment of self-annoyance. He had not intended to kill an innocent creature and thus spoil the perfection of the place where he had found peace. He had kicked the door ajar and was now powerless to close it.

"How many times have I done this?" the man thought wearily. "How many times have I destroyed life around me?" His heart throbbed in his throat. It seemed as though his children were stuck there, with a host of others whom he had hurt through his preferred ignorance. It was this he had hoped to escape by embarking on his quest. But it had come back to remind him, in the form of a lowly worm.

An earthworm did not mean much to him, except as a symbol of how he had fallen short of his own expectations, perhaps, and for this the worm had died. Was it a fair exchange, the worm's life for the man's momentary self-reproach? He threw the corpse back to the earth. He did not think that other worms would feed someday on his own body. He thought with a sigh, "I must go on."

But as he continued upward through the afternoon sun, sweating, straining always upward, he began to realize just how difficult it would be to attain the transformation he sought. Such a transformation did not come as a gift. It would not occur merely because he desired it. Even the act of leaving all and putting his body on the upward path did not suffice. Something else had to happen, something he did not yet know about. Vaguely, that something else tugged at him in the wish to die, to end it all, to finish this chapter forever, to come full circle.

But the mountain was there, in his throat, under his feet. And the higher he got the fuller his heart beat in his throat. Perhaps he would never learn the secrets of self-transformation. Perhaps his life would be a life of trying, trying, finally consummating itself in a death un-tried-for.

Sometime during the afternoon he reached the point of no return. It came to him, as he rested in the shade of an outcropping and looked out over the valley below, that he could not go back. Home was too far away. The only way to get back home was to climb the mountain.

He watched the afternoon shadows stride across the distant valley and the mountains beyond. Through the sweat stinging his eyes the landscape seemed to shimmer and dance, its ruddy face beguiling the sun. It seemed alien to him.

Something had got into his blood. Perhaps it was the rigor and adventure of the quest itself. Perhaps it was desperation. Whatever it was, he found himself preferring to be lost for the time, to be scarred by the rock and blistered by the sun. He preferred the dust and the glare, the sharp, hot smell of sage and the terror of distance. He preferred the barren, eroded soil, the shape of cactus and stone, the shadow of the blue-black raven that hovered above him, reminding him that death itself was also on a quest, that it was starving and had nothing to eat. His belly cried out to be filled. His throat cried out to be emptied. His being cried out to be transformed. Above him the raven circled, clacked its beak and hoarsely croaked.

Nightfall found the tired man on a shoulder of the mountain. For the last few hours he had followed what seemed to be a faint trail that headed in the general direction he wished to travel. The trail terminated amid a pile of basalt that appeared to have been placed there by human hands, forming a rough semi-circle against the northwest. Down on the ground he found faint traces of ash from an old fire. It seemed a good place to spend the night.

Close by he found fuel: pungent sage and fragrant juniper. With his hands he dug a firepit, scooping the sandy soil into his lap. The simple ritual of building it gave him pleasure – the placement of stone into a sculpture to serve his need.

As night fell, his fire climbed. Hungry light leaped for the darkness, for his eyes. Again, he experienced a sense of deep satisfaction. Below his hunger for a new life there was a deeper hunger, symbolized by the sinuous flames of his fire. Ceaselessly he burned, perched in the pyre of his crumbling bones. To do what? To give off warmth and light.

He sat back against a boulder and watched the evening star bathe herself in reflected light. He longed for the source of the reflection. The small fire carved a cave in the darkness. Save for the sputtering flame, silence was absolute.

He must have dozed off. When he opened his eyes again, a human-like figure was silently sitting opposite him.

The man gave a start of surprise, leaping suddenly to his feet, scattering the fire. An involuntary exclamation exploded from his lips. But the figure did not move nor speak nor look up from its lap. Closer attention revealed that the sudden guest was a male Indian of indeterminate age with long, black hair and a broad-brimmed, silver-banded black hat. Despite a pair of rabbit skin moccasins, he was not otherwise dressed as a Native American, but as a white man, in blue jeans and a rough, white workshirt.

More cautious than frightened now, the man returned to the fire. "Who are you?" he asked the dark figure staring at his hands in his lap. "Why are you here?"

"My name is 'The Cutter.' You camp in my camp by my fire," said the form, looking up without a trace of malice. "You are welcome to sit here and be warm."

The man realized his visitor was incorporeal. What passed as a human figure was a bright mass of fleshy pools and shadows that shifted and flowed. Glittering, dark, rainbow eyes measured him. The man fought an intense desire to flee; but the terms of his own quest again compelled him to remain and to learn whatever the apparition's presence in his life required of him.

"Forgive me for intruding," he said. "I had hoped to spend the night here and in the morning to resume my quest."

The apparition that referred to itself as "The Cutter" wavered, then held steady. The fire sputtered. Finally the dark form spoke. "This mountain belongs to 'The People.'"

"Who are 'The People?'"

"My people are The People," the apparition replied. "Your people will pass away when the winter is past. I wait here for the return of spring and The People." A screech owl trembled the night air. The Cutter looked away, into the night and said nothing.

The man ventured another question of the ghost. "Why do you call yourself The Cutter?"

"My white name is Jack Wilson. I am also called 'The Christ.' When I was a grown man I was taken up into the heart of heaven. I was there forever. I learned the secret of bringing The People back. I learned how to cut, to split apart, to sever. I brought back peace and I brought back an axe, with which to cut away, to make clear and ready. I live to make a way for The People to return."

There was a long pause. The Cutter took from his belt a circular, flat, polished, black object. He held it up to the light of the fire. It was an obsidian mirror. "It cuts away lies. Look," he commanded, and passed the object to the white man.

In the dull light of the fire the wondrous mirror softly glowed. The man looked into the black, lustrous reflection. He saw a little boy who was starving and had nothing to eat. His body was frail, his soul was innocent. A shock of blond hair topped a guileless face holding a tentative smile. "Do you like me?" he seemed to be asking. The little boy was none other than the man himself, when he was a boy. Astonished, the man turned to the apparition.

"You are a man growing older," The Cutter said. "You are really a little boy growing younger. Soon the little boy will die."

For a long time the man could not speak. He experienced a great sadness. The heart of his childhood that his mother had given him mourned in his aching throat and made it impossible to speak. He was afraid. He wanted to be with his mother. He did not understand death. He did not want to be set adrift on the sea of life. His boat was frail. Inevitably it would sink. He did not want to accept the responsibility of death.

"I will tell you a story," said the apparition. A great sensation of pain, like a wave, seemed to overwhelm him. "It is the story of the Ghost Dance."*

---

*The apparition is a real personage, and the tale that follows is derived from historical accounts of the Ghost Dance Religion, a late nineteenth-century messianic movement founded by the Paiute prophet Wovoka, sometimes called the Indian Christ. See *Bury My Heart at Wounded Knee*, Dee Brown. The sequence of Ghost Dance songs that follow are quoted or adapted from *Technicians of the Sacred*, Jerome Rothenberg, ed.

156

"When I returned from Heaven I saw far and clear. I became a prophet and a teacher among my people. I sent out messages to all the Nations. I said, Come and meet me here at Walker River where the white man has put me. I sent out my message: Salvation is at hand. We will be delivered from the white man. Come and dance the dance of salvation. Come and learn to dance the Ghost Dance.

"From everywhere Indians came to hear and to see. Many Nations came, for many were living by the hand of the white man instead of the hand of God, and they were starving and had nothing to eat. The buffalo were gone. Birds fell from the sky, too rotten to be eaten. The snows came. The Indian's tongue was frozen to the white man's axe.

"I said, Everyone come. Learn to dance the Ghost Dance. Indians everywhere must dance and keep on dancing. Pretty soon, when spring returns, God will return. God will bring back the fish and the game. I said, If you keep on dancing your mothers and fathers and grandmothers and grandfathers will return and the earth will be young again.

"I said, The white man will be cut down like grass in the fire. Rains will tear his house into the oceans. Fire will rain from the sky and burn his bones to ash. I said, The white man will be eaten by the forest; the earth will swallow him. All Indians must keep on dancing and the white man will die, chopped and burned as if by a stroke of lightning. O my People, I cried, the winter is cold. Let us dance so that spring will come!

"These things I taught, and the Nations came and listened, and believed. They learned to dance the Ghost Dance. They went back to their people and taught them also how to dance the Ghost Dance. Soon many people of many Nations were dancing the Ghost Dance.

"But the white man saw. First he was disturbed. Then he was frightened. He saw Indians dancing. In the terrible dead cold of winter he saw Indians dancing.

"'No!' said the white man. 'You cannot dance here. You disturb my dreams; you disturb my conscience. I am afraid of you because I took your land away from you by force. You cannot, you *must not* dance this dance.'

"The Indians went away to another place and kept on dancing. In his dreams the white man heard the drumming of their feet and he was afraid for his life. He came with many big guns and soldiers and ordered my people to stop dancing. But my people would not stop dancing. They were dancing to make the white man go away. He could not allow them to dance. With his soldiers and big guns he killed my people. He slaughtered them in cold blood, even the women and children. Even the dogs. They died like the rabbit, like the fish, trapped, hunted down. The snow was stained with the blood of my people.

"And every bullet that found its mark was a nail that crucified me to the white man's cross. With every bullet that found its mark I died again.

"But let me tell you, white man," the ghost said with a curiously warm and gentle intonation, "I am not dead. I am risen. And the Ghost Dance goes on."

The wind stirred the fire, the stars cast their cold brilliance. All was silent. The flame died into coals. The man reached to throw more wood on the fire, suddenly afraid of the darkness. He had felt, more than heard, what the apparition of The Cutter had said to him and now he was empty and cold.

The ghost resumed. "You ask me what is the meaning of your life. You ask me to teach you how to let go of one world so that you may attain a better one. You ask me to be your guide to the sacred mountain. I tell you that you must learn to dance the Ghost Dance and to keep on dancing, for winter is hard and you are starving and have nothing to eat. Come, white man. You will learn to dance the Ghost Dance."

The apparition of the man who taught the Nations how to die by dancing shifted from the fire and became seemingly corporeal off to the side where there was room to move about. Then he began to dance in a circle, shuffling his feet in a coherent, rudimentary rhythm. And as he danced he sang a song. The song was simple and powerful.

We shall live again.
We shall live again.

Something within the questing man responded, something that was deeply sorrowing, something that was full of joy. The little boy in the mirror tugged at the heart in his throat. Let us dance, said the little boy, so that the evil of the world will go away. Let us dance, proud in ourselves and sure that spring will return, that we shall live again. Let us dance with the heat of the sun, for I am afraid of the dark and my mother's breasts are cold.

In a twinkling, spring had yielded to summer, summer to fall, and fall to winter. The world was dying, smothered in chilling, deadly white, the color of the white man. The springs were frozen, the pinyon were rotting, the eagle had no hope, the rabbit was sick, The People were starving. There was a man who had been to Heaven who said the only hope for all was to dance the Ghost Dance, and to keep on dancing, for surely spring would come.

The white man arose and began to dance. And after a while he sang his song, the song his children and the rattlesnake and the worm had taught him, the song of his heart yearning for spring.

> Great Spirit, have mercy on me.
> I am starving, I have nothing to eat.

And the two danced on, as the fire grew dim and the cold numbed the darkness. The white man felt his body become the body of humankind. His heart, as it pounded and whirled in his throat, caused him to moan and cry out, to reach God, to be God.

And then the night was pierced again by the ghost, who sang a new song in a ringing voice that sounded like the rush of water from beneath a snow bank.

> In the great night
> My heart will go out
> Toward me the darkness comes rattling
> In the great night
> My heart will go out

The firelight faded. Darkness surrounded and took possession of the dance. The presence of the two dancing forms became measureless, invisible. All that mattered was the pounding of the darkness through the feet of the earth, the whirling of stars in the mind of the night sky. From the darkness of this ecstasy came a voice that spoke through the heart in the throat of the white man.

> The earth will tremble
> Everyone will arise
> Stretch out your hands.

Something was stirring in the darkness, in the hoarse panting, in the letting go, in the insensate knowing of the dance. Was it a seed of perfect silence sown to the winds of motion? Was it a moment of undying truth? In the dead of darkness, light was singing. And it was this light that took the form of the dance. The same light shone from the hearts of all peoples and drew them together into the One Dance, which was being danced by the earth, the night, and the light of the stars.

Light stirred in the heart of darkness, in the tomb of the seed, in the dung of the beetle, in the fang of the rattlesnake, in the pumping hearts of man and ghost until neither could be distinguished from the other, until their substance received the darkness and the earth and stars and their spirits were born as one and a voice sang one last endless song.

This earth too old
Trees too old
Our lives too old
All will be new again
All will be new again

When the white man could no longer dance he fell lengthward, toward the unrisen dawn.

When again he opened his eyes he was not sure he had ever closed them. No time had elapsed. He was still dancing the Ghost Dance to the light of the fire in his veins.

Gradually he became aware that he was lying in the hard dust. Morning had broken in upon the night. In the morning light all perspective had changed. The Cutter was gone. The ashes of the fire lay inert and cold. But the earth on which the white man lay was pounded into a circular groove, apparently by dancing, shuffling feet. All the footprints belonged to him.

The white man felt alert, at ease and ready for what must surely come. The terms of his dream of quest had brought him to a final reckoning. From the start he had known, deep inside, that he must face it.

A croak from above reminded him, as if he should forget, that the raven was still sitting up there, waiting on the air. He hoisted his pack to his shoulders and began the last day of his climb.

160

He felt amazingly whole, strong enough to look his mountain in the eye. His body moved with ease and freedom, accommodating gravity. Details of the landscape stood out with peculiar clarity, every stone and bush, every tree and gully, every new perspective on the valley below – the habitations of the white man, the life he had left behind.

His feet lifted him steadily. At noon he stopped to rest in the shade of a pinyon. He had been climbing an arroyo punctuated by intermittent springs. Patches of maidenhair fern clung to wet rocks. Willows were budding and thistles putting out their purple and yellow stars. Bees and hummingbirds sang on the air. Once he startled a doe, coming downwind of her. He was surprised at how silently he had been able to approach her. Heavy with child, she was sleek and wide-eyed.

He basked for a while in the sweet wind, looking ahead. The outer curve of the shoulder of the mountain obscured the peak. The way continued to be steep. Ahead lay barren highlands, with an occasional pinyon or whitebark pine, twisted and scoured by the winds. This was no country for faint hearts. The uplands were bare and exposed. Nowhere was there shelter. Trees could not grow here without paying the awful price of slow, agonized adaption and growth. The air was thin, rarefied. The sky had turned a deeper blue. Ahead lay pockets of snow and the wind-besieged heights.

Sinking into the shade of the pinyon, he lay his head on his arm and heaved a sigh. Always the upward pull against the current. The factor of work. Surely, there was a joy to this work. For a long time he listened to the beating of the heart in his throat, steady and hot. His very blood seemed to be answering his weariness with a resolute energy. Tired as he was, he knew he would gain the summit before nightfall.

A small object on a branch caught his eye. He looked closer. A small, ruby-throated hummingbird, silent and still as any pebble. Was it asleep? He went closer. No, it was dead.

To the man who stroked it, the feathered little shell was a symbol of the way of all life. In the corpse he saw mirrored his own body and recognized that there is something in beauty that lives on, that survives, that is born again in a higher, transcendent dimension. Thus his dying heart pulled him forward, to some hoped-for death or culmination at the summit of the mountain, to the unveiling of the treasure.

By evening he had reached the summit. It was barren and rocky, crusted with ancient, wind-scoured dolomite. There were no trees here. There were no bushes, no boulders among which to find shelter. There was only the bulge of the mountain and the surrounding sky.

The view was magnificent. To the east he could see a hundred miles: desolation and wilderness, expanse, *las sierras desiertas,* the crests of the ranges of the Great Basin. To the west, in the rays of the setting sun, lay a composition of dark angles and contours and shadowed hulks: *La Sierra Nevada,* the saw-teeth of snow. Slowly the sun was quitting the habitations of day.

Out there somewhere were his wife and children, his parents and friends, his people, his work, his life. He pictured that universe and loved it with great feeling, from a great distance. What are they doing now? he wondered, and pictured them sitting down to dinner or driving home along the highway. He longed to be with them. He longed to be without them. He loved them for themselves; he loved them for who they wanted to be. He felt their presence in him, strong and warming in the darkening wind.

From his lofty purchase he contemplated for a moment the human condition, the beauty and the tragedy of it, the aching and throbbing in the heart of humanity. But quickly he became bored with his own philosophy. His quest required doing, not contemplation.

He set about the task of constructing a circle of stones to protect himself from the night wind. Somewhere in a book he had seen pictures of circles made by primitive peoples for the same reason. Carrying and placing the rough dolomite proved to be hard work, but he was pleased with the results. He would lie curled up inside his circle of stones, like a baby, like an old man, hugging himself and the earth, and wait for what the night would bring him. Darkness was coming and darkness was starving and had nothing to eat.

The last light hung to the western horizon like a purple curtain. The silhouettes of mountains higher than the one he had climbed etched the distance like great stepping stones. And then from the east night came, climbing the mountains as silently and effortlessly as light, until it had conquered all.

He entered the circle and lay against the stony soil. Still the wind blew cold. He huddled up tight, covered himself with a blanket, his back to the wind. He had not realized it would be so cold, that he would be miserable. Where was the triumph?

He shut his eyes tight against the shivers and tried to unclench the core of himself. He felt tired and sick and afraid. Yet in the extremity of his exhaustion he could not sleep nor overcome his fear of exposure and the cold. He realized that he was panting, that his heart was beating faster than normal, distending his throat with an ache, a desire to cry endlessly.

He looked up at the stars. Familiar and alien, menacing and compelling, the stars gripped his body with their ancient spell and told him a tale he would never understand. His bones ached, his feet were cold. He was a long way from home, lonely and alone. He had taken himself beyond the hearing of any other human. He was lost.

He began to question his actions. "What am I doing here? I climbed this mountain – for what? I left my wife and children behind – for what? Here I am, cold and miserable, atop the illusory dream. I have worked hard to get here. It has been a lifetime. Where is the fulfillment of the promise? Where is the precious treasure? Where is God? Where is the Great Spirit?" The stars watched impassively.

What a fool I am, he thought bitterly, to believe that those who hunger shall be filled. He pitied and belittled himself, and for a long time stared vacantly at the newly-risen moon, overwhelmed by a sense of failure. What had his life amounted to? When he was young he had entertained dreams of greatness. He was going to be somebody, a servant of humanity, a hero, a Great Teacher. As he grew older his dreams had faded into the obscurity of his lived experience. There might be heroes, but he was not one of them.

But even in the midst of his average, day-to-day existence, even when he knew all too well his imperfection and impotence, he had hoped that someday he would be more complete, more fulfilled by his life. That hope had brought him to the summit of the Mountain of the Heart. But now that he was here, where was *here?* He felt no joy in having successfully climbed the mountain. Night was upon him. He feared the meanness and smallness of his own life. Whatever gain he had won on the approach to the mountain was lost to him now, swept away by the winds of self-doubt.

A poignant solitude pervaded the universe of the great mountain atop which crouched a tiny figure encircled by stones. Was this the meaning of life, this unquenchable, empty loneliness? Was this the gift of life, this separation from the mother, this freedom to be filled with despair and longing for what one can neither know nor express?

Perhaps the universe heard him. The chill wind subsided. Silence and deep darkness pervaded the mountain. He lay in his grave of stones and fell into a profound reverie, punctuated only by the sound of his heartbeat and heavy breathing. For a long time he ceased to think or feel and went away to a place where Nothing ruled. He became invisible to the cold, indifferent to himself and the night of stars. He forgot the dimension of time. Neither asleep nor awake, he existed as if he were suspended in no-space, no-time. He was somewhere. He was nowhere.

But the wind spoke again and startled him from his eternity. The wind was starving, starving for his body, starving for his attention. It seethed between the stones of his circle and shook him from his Nothing Dream, saying: "Here we are, you and I. Here we are."

The wind spoke so clearly that he might even have heard it in his mind's ear. He groaned back at it, from his numbed and aching body.

"I want to die."

"Then die," sang the wind.

"How?"

"Let go, let go," moaned the wind.

"But I *have* let go."

"Let go of it all. Let go of yourself," cried the wind.

"How?"

"Mother, mother, mother," whispered the wind. "Go to your mother."

"But my mother is dead."

"Your mother is not dead. Your mother lives forever."

So sang the gentle, cruel, wise, impatient spirit of the night wind. And the man heard. In his cold misery of wanting to die he heard the wisdom of the wind and knew what he had to do there in the brooding darkness.

Ignited by the keening of the starving, desolate wind, an aching longing to go home, to go home to mother, seized him. If only he could curl up against her breast and feel her holding him up, warm and steady. He could not endure their separation any longer. He would go back to the source, to the place from whence he had come, for he was sick of himself, sick of his life, sick of his incompleteness, sick of being separate from that which he desired deep in his earthen body.

It seemed for a moment the image of his mortal mother passed before him again, as she had in the cave. His father also appeared and the two of them were young and vibrant. It was their wedding day. She was in a bridal gown and held a wreath. He was in a dark suit and held her hand. The two of them appeared so innocent of any knowledge of what they later became: old and tired and ailing.

He loved them with the longing of one who would never see them again. He wanted to tell them that he loved them, that he wished them well, that he hoped they would find their life treasure. "I was one of their treasures," he thought, "their first born son." The thought made him want to be worthy of them, to do what he was to do with bravery and grace, to live this one night perfectly atop the mountain of his dreams.

The two images remained, silent, before him, symbols of foreverness, symbols of change and death. He did not speak to them. His heart throbbed in his throat, contending with feelings too deep for words. And then they were gone. He let them go. Somehow, they lived in him already, were married in him. The force of their spiritual vow he carried in his bones and blood and in the fiber of his soul.

He said goodbye to them, as if for the last time, and sat upright in his circle, looking into the nothingness. Then his wife and children came to him, his life as a husband and father.

He had loved many women before he loved his wife. But he had loved her best and finally. It had not been she, nor any other person, who was responsible for his restless searching for a vision. She trusted him and gave him courage, took him for what he was and gave him to his dreams.

Remembrance of the richness and the beauty of his life with his wife and children suffused him. He could not recall the depression and anxiety that had led him to the top of the mountain. Surely I am incomplete, he thought, not to have seen the completeness of my life. Certain moments he had spent with them would let any man die happily. He wondered: Why was I unable to enjoy my life, to see the beauty in it?

But down inside he knew why. Because he had been unhappy with himself. He had carried his life around like a burden. Why did he climb the mountain? Not because he wanted to be more than who he was, but because he wanted to lose himself so that he could find himself. If losing himself meant that he must die, then he would die.

Suddenly he was struck by an extraordinary truth. Dying does not mean leaving loved ones behind, for all are united in the great Mother Heart. "I cannot leave those I love behind, for all are bound together by love and love is stronger than death." He thought this thought and trembled with fear; he had so little faith.

Outside the circle of his laboring thoughts the substance of things held steady, as it does without beginning or end. The night persisted. The darkness of the grave, the crypt, the vault, the hidden and secret, the mysterious and fecund, pervaded the night. Out across the Great Basin and west to the Ocean of Peace the night *was*. And somewhere in it was the feeble spark of consciousness that was the man who wanted to lose himself and go home to his mother.

That spark of consciousness was a seed—a seed that could not break forth from its corpse until it had gone back to the dark, star-filled vulva of the Mother Heart. The rattlesnake, the worm, the mesquite tree, the humming-bird, the prophet Wovoka, were they not all seeds that hungered to return to the Mother Heart and shared with him the hope of being united with her? And did these seeds not obey, with thousands of years of obedience, the heartbeat of the source that conceived and sent them forth into an outward-ness that was always and eternally a returning, a coming home?

Whatever strength he had won by being weak, whatever hope he had salvaged from a heap of broken dreams, whatever faith he possessed from a life of doubt, whatever love was left in his bitter cup of breath, began to fill his heart. But the reservoir would never be filled, nor would it ever run dry. And his heart's cry unto the Mother Heart continued to pierce the night: "Have mercy on me. I am starving and have nothing to eat."

His being went out to all the creatures and spirits of the earth, in a flood of empathy: We are all separate and alone and yet we share the same origin, the same flesh, the same mind, the same destination. Our hearts beat in unison. We have all endured the painful labor of separation and growth. Severed from our mother, we wander the earth, starving, looking for our home. Lonely, we seek oneness with our kind, and though we wake apart and die apart, in waking we take root in our Mother; in dying we sow our seeds to the wind and go back to her.

He let go of his life and let the wind carry him out into the darkness across the moonlit crags and crests of the eastern mountains. His heart was a seed winging its way to the meadowlands of the mountain of the heart. The wind pierced him with cold, bright song. It buoyed him up, as though his soul were a boat setting forth on an unknown journey. For a moment he felt a twinge of regret, a nostalgia for the beauty of the life that had been. But then he yielded his heart to his Mother and the little boy, free of his aging, tired flesh, ran home.

Like the rustle of wings, the light of dawn began to beat its heart against the east. The moon paled. The mountain in the desert reared up to the rosy sky, and a tiny form atop its summit stirred and looked up. As the clear water of dawn cleaved the stone of darkness, so the man came forth from the night, wide-eyed and fresh, eager to see and know. The treasure he had come for lay shimmering just below the edge of the horizon. He knew it. His crystal-cold body could feel it: the stirring of life. A cosmic upwelling of emotion filled and then overflowed him. He tried to sing, but his heart was still in his throat. Is this the treasure? he wondered, and laughed. Then he cried, like a baby.

For abruptly, illuminating his red, grizzled, bawling face and casting the first shadow as far as eternity, thundered the sun, throbbing light into the world like a beating, bursting heart. As it consumed the night with its thunder-arrows of desire, it sang a song. The song was: "Great Mother have mercy on me. I am starving. I have nothing to eat."

What we look for beyond seeing
And call the unseen,
Listen for beyond hearing
And call the unheard,
Grasp for beyond reaching
And call the withheld,
Merge beyond understanding
In a oneness
Which does not merely rise and give light,
Does not merely set and leave darkness,
But forever sends forth a succession of living
   things as mysterious
As the unbegotten existence to which they return.
—Lao Tzu, The Way of Life

Contributors in Order of Appearance

Creosote: Dr. Mark Stillman, Last Chance Mountains
I'd Pick a Daisy: Gerry Goodwin, Inyo Mountains
Companion of the Wind: Eric Baker, White Mountains
Free Bird: Jennie Oppenheimer, Starvation Canyon, Death Valley
Weak Stomach, Strong Heart: Annette Wire, Starvation Canyon, Death Valley
Moon Song Crying: Eric Knudsen, Upper Reese River, Nevada
Lone Stone Among the Rest: Sue Amon, Black Mountains, Death Valley
Linda: Linda Gregory, Cerro Colorado, Baja California Sur
Keenan: Keenan Foster, White Mountains
Fire Stick: Rich Kerkorian, White Mountains
Gift Bearer: Virginia Hine, Saline Mountains
Solo: Natalie Rogers, Funeral Mountains, Death Valley
Mark: Mark O'Neill, Panamint Mountains, Death Valley
Ruth: Sister Ruth Wallin, Panamint Mountains, Death Valley
Listens With the Heart: Sister Patricia Burke, Panamint Mountains,
      Death Valley
Looking Into the Fire: Marilyn Riley, Hunter Mountain, Death Valley
Lonely Heart Outreaching: Meredith Little, Saline Mountains
Broken Heart Laughing: Willie Stapp, *bahia de la concepcion*, Baja California Sur
Rock: Howard Voskuyl, Saline Mountains
Trisha: Trisha Bishop, Starvation Canyon, Death Valley
Little Warrior: Steve de Martini, South Warner Wilderness
Glowing Mountain in the Dawn: Claudia Dunlavy, Black Mountains,
      Death Valley
Silence: Jack Crimmins, Caribou Wilderness

Annotated
Bibliography

Those who wish to become more acquainted with the philosophical, mythological, anthropological, psychological and religious concepts undergirding this book will find this descriptive bibliography to be of use. The works listed below are not intended to be representative of available literature on the subject. Rather they are indicative of the author's search for a meaningful rite of passage experience for people facing life crises.

Abbey, Edward, *Desert Solitaire,* New York, McGraw-Hill.

> This book has no direct bearing on Vision Questing, but is one of the best ever written on the subject of the desert, an environment admirably suited to Vision Questing. As Mr. Abbey maintains, the desert is an awful place. Who would ever want to go there?

Anonymous, *Mysteries of the Seed,* Tlálpam, Mexico, Ediciones del Sol, 1954.

> A mysterious little book written as though the author were an eyewitness to the rituals of the ancient Elusian Mysteries. It contains the injunction to the candidates: "Unlearn your human thoughts and face your solitude."

The Bible, Old and New Testaments.

> The Judeo-Christian tradition includes many tales of prophets who went into the wilderness and brought back vision to their people.

Blake, William, *Complete Writings,* London, Oxford, 1966.

> The wisdom of Blake points the way for all who seek "To see a world in a grain of sand / And a heaven in a wild flower."

Bly, Robert, *Sleepers Joining Hands*, New York, Harper and Row, 1973.

We came forth from the Great Mother and we will return to the Great Mother. Nowhere can be found a more cogent and clear telling of this story than in Bly's essay, "I Came Out of the Mother Naked."

Brown, Joseph Epes, *The Sacred Pipe: The Seven Rites of the Oglala Sioux*, Norman, University of Oklahoma Press, 1953.

Told to Brown over a period of time by Black Elk, this book of sacred rites contains the great holy man's description of the *Hanblecheyapi*, or "crying for a vision" rite by which young men among the Oglala Sioux attained adult status.

Campbell, Joseph, *Hero With a Thousand Faces*, New York, Bollingen, 1949.

This popular treatise on the meaning of mythology synergizes all myth into a mono-myth, and makes the heroic accessible to modern consciousness.

Castaneda, Carlos, *Journey to Ixtlan*, New York, Simon and Schuster, 1972.

The apprentice is prepared by Don Juan and Don Genaro, then goes alone to a sacred "power place."

Eliade, Mircea, *From Primitives to Zen*, New York, Harper and Row, 1967.

This anthology of religious texts represents a wide spectrum of myths and ritual practices from ancient to modern times. Material is arranged according to theme.

Eliot, T. S., *Complete Poems and Plays*, New York, Harcourt, 1958.

Certain poems, "The Waste Land," "The Hollow Men," "Ash Wednesday," and "The Four Quartets," immortalize the erosion of traditional myth by the irresistible forces of science and modern technology. Eliot seeks redemption at "the still point of the turning world" where mystical insight is born.

Evans-Wentz, W. Y., *The Tibetan Book of the Dead,* New York, Oxford, 1960.

> The message of this ancient book of instruction on the Art of Dying is that the Art of Dying is very similar to the Art of Coming into Birth.

Hall, Manley Palmer, *The Secret Teachings of All Ages,* Los Angeles, The Philosophical Research Society, 1969.

> An encyclopedia replete with rituals, allegories, myths, and mysteries of many philosophical and religious movements from the beginning of history. It is a rich source for those who seek symbols with which to create their own rituals.

Harding, M. Esther, *Woman's Mysteries: Ancient and Modern.* New York, Harper and Row, 1971.

> This intelligent book sets about reinstating the feminine principle, as symbolized by the ancient rites of the moon, in individual modern life.

Jung, C. G., *The Collected Works,* New York, Pantheon, 1953–.

> Perhaps Jung's greatest contribution to modern thought is his contention that in order to effect a constructive and lasting change in our lives we must transform ourselves with archetype and myth.

Mooney, James, *The Ghost-Dance Religion and the Sioux Outbreak of 1890,* Fourteenth Annual Report, Part 2, Bureau of American Ethnology (Washington, D.C., 1896).

> This Native American messianic movement was born among the Paiute (the "water guardians"), the true inhabitants of the area in which the majority of the Vision Quests have taken place. The central message of the Ghost Dance was the disappearance of the white man, the regeneration of the spirit of the Indian, and the regeneration of the earth.

Pinkson, Tom, *A Quest for Vision,* San Francisco, Freeperson Press, 1976.

This book breaks new soil. It is about junkies, speed freaks, vision, psychological ecology, and the Great Spirit. It also contains a description of the first modern Vision Quest attempted in Marin County.

Rothenberg, Jerome, *Technicians of the Sacred,* New York, Doubleday, 1968.

This rich, versatile anthology links poetry and ritual on a primitive (complex) level and points to sources of ritual poetics in the modern world.

Sheehy, Gail, *Passages: Predictable Crises of Adult Life,* New York, Dutton, 1976.

The author remarks on the need for modern individuals facing midlife crises to find a way to formalize or mark their transition. Needless to say, the same is true of adolescents who face the crises of transition from childhood to adulthood.

Storm, Hyemeyohsts, *Seven Arrows,* New York, Harper and Row, 1972.

This beautiful, wise book written by a Cheyenne shield maker contains fables, stories, and rites of great importance to the study of the Vision Quest.

Van der Post, Laurens, *A Story Like the Wind, A Far Off Place,* London, Hogarth Press, 1972, 1974.

About the passage of a boy into manhood in the African bush, these two novels recreate the heart and soul and instinctive, whole complexity of the ways of the first people, the bushmen of the Kalahari Desert.

Van Gennep, Arnold, *The Rites of Passage,* Chicago, University of Chicago Press, 1960.

Van Gennep was the first anthropologist to note the regularity, significance, and function of rites attached to transitional stages in human life.

About the Authors

Steven Foster, Ph.D., and Meredith Little are directors of The School of Lost Borders, Big Pine, CA, a ceremonial and training facility of wilderness initiation form and process. Formerly Associate Professor of Humanities at San Francisco State University, Dr. Foster co-founded and directed (with Meredith Little) Rites of Passage, Inc., Marin County, CA, for eight years.

Meredith Little, a graduate in Human Responsibility of Antioch College West, is formerly a trainer at Marin Suicide Prevention and Crisis Intervention Center.

They are also authors of *Passing from Childhood to Adulthood: A Coursebook for Graduating Seniors* (Rites of Passage Press) and *The Sacred Mountain: A Vision Quest Handbook for Adults* (Rites of Passage Press). They are the associate editors of *Betwixt and Between: Patterns of Masculine and Feminine Initiation* (Open Court Press, Louise Mahdi, editor), and are writing *The Roaring of the Sacred River: Modern Apprenticeship to an Ancient Ceremony of Passage*. They are married and are raising two children. Much of their time is spent in the deserts of the Great Basin. They are members of the Society of Indian Psychologists and the California Native Plant Society.